Papa Bear's Favorite Italian Dishes

Papa Bear's Favorite Italian Dishes

Father Joseph Orsini

LOGOS INTERNATIONAL
Plainfield, N.J.

I wish to thank Mrs. Ann Hughes who encouraged me to write a cookbook.

I thank the good Lord who placed me in such a wonderful family and gave me such beautiful friends.

I thank Mrs. Pat Heintz who so patiently typed from my handwritten manuscript.

PAPA BEAR'S FAVORITE ITALIAN DISHES
Copyright © 1976 by Logos International. All rights reserved.
Printed in the United States of America.
International Standard Book Number: 0-88270-127-4 (Hardcover)
0-88270-316-1 (Softcover)
Library of Congress Catalog Card Number: 75-7479
Logos International, Plainfield, NJ 07061

To my mother, Carmela Orsini, who not only taught me how to cook but how to love.

Contents

Biography

The Reverend Doctor Joseph E. Orsini was born in Bayonne, New Jersey, June 1, 1937, to Carmela and the now deceased Giuseppe Orsini.

His noteworthy scholastic career began as an honor graduate of St. Anthony's High School, Jersey City, N.J. in June, 1956.

He went on to earn the Bachelor of Arts degree magna cum laude in the field of classical languages from Seton Hall University, South Orange, N.J. in 1960 and was awarded the Cross and Crescent for academic excellence.

He completed his theological studies at St. John's Seminary, Little Rock, Arkansas, where he held the post of professor of Latin and Italian for four years. He was ordained to the priesthood in Camden, N.J., May 16, 1964.

He earned the MA degree from Seton Hall University in the field of Secondary Education in 1965, magna cum laude.

He earned the Doctor's Degree in the Philosophy of Education from Rutgers University in May, 1973.

Since ordination he has served the following parishes as associate pastor in residence: St. Isidore, Vineland, N.J., Sacred Heart, Mt. Ephraim, N.J., Mt. Carmel, Camden, N.J., St. Paul, Stone Harbor, N.J., St. Agnes, Blackwood, N.J., St. John, Collingswood, N.J., Assumption, Bayonne, N.J., and St. Edward, Pine Hill, N.J.

During the years since ordination, he has been on the faculties of the following schools as teacher of Latin, French, English, Religion and Philosophy: Camden Catholic High School, Cherry Hill, N.J., Paul VI High School, Haddon Heights, N.J., and presently, Gloucester Catholic High School, Gloucester City, N.J. From Sept. 1970 to Jan. 1971 he held the professorship in the Department of Modern Religious Education at Don Bosco College, Newton, N.J.

Father Orsini has written many articles of cultural and religious interest in Unico National Magazine and Logos Journal. He has produced two religious best sellers in his books, *Hear My Confession* and *The Anvil*, published by Logos International, Plainfield, N.J.

He has served Unico National, a service organization of Italian-American business and professional men, as National Chaplain since 1965 and received their award for distinguished service in 1967. Marquis Who's Who Inc. selected him to be a biographer for the 15th edition of *Who's Who in the East*.

Introduction

I have been an amateur chef ever since I could reach my mother's kitchen stove. In fact the first time I reached for the stove was when I was four years old. My mother was preparing Pastina Al Burro (tiny macaroni boiled in salted water and seasoned with butter—a typical dish prepared by Italian mothers for their tots) and as she looked away, I reached up to see what was in the pot. In a second, my first encounter with the stove became a disaster. I spilled the contents all over me and suffered third degree burns on my left arm. That didn't discourage me though, for a few years later, I did the same thing, on the same arm, with a pot of hot coffee. You would think I would quit after that, but being a stubborn little Calabrese (the people who come from my parents' region of Italy-Calabria, are famous for being *teste dure* i.e., hard-headed stubborn individuals), I persisted. My first career with the stove began in my late teens when I took up the hobby of baking. I baked cookies, cakes, pies and pizzas at every opportunity I could get. I was getting pretty good at it, but Mamma put a stop to it. I was a great baker but a lousy cleaner-upper. After cleaning up behind me for some time, Mamma decided it was cheaper to buy in the bakery. That ended that.

Some time later, I began cooking in earnest. It was really a matter of survival. I was in the seminary in Little Rock, Arkansas, and this Italian kid just couldn't cope with mustard greens and grits. I went from a 206 lb. weakling to a 140 lb. weakling in one year. That year, thanks to corn flakes and peanut butter, I barely managed to stay alive. When I arrived home for summer vacation my mother kept on looking for the fat kid she sent to Arkansas with a supply of dried sausage. Now her kid *looked* like a dried sausage. Mamma made up her mind to formulate a survival plan. During the following years her "Care" packages arrived for me at the seminary at regular intervals. The packages were filled with familiar Italian foodstuffs. I would carefully unload them when no one was around, and by trial and error, mostly error, I learned to cook. Around my cooking adventures there grew a select "secret" society of fellow seminarians, mostly from the East Coast, who willingly became the guinea pigs for my attempts at Italian cooking. They're all still alive and kicking, and so am I, so I guess it wasn't so bad.

When I was ordained a priest and traveled from parish assignment to parish assignment, I always found a sympathetic family who allowed me to use their kitchen to perfect my expertise. Today, even Mamma says I'm a pretty good cook, so I guess I've earned the right to write this book.

I've called this little volume *Papa Bear's Favorite Italian Dishes*. That calls for some explanation. My last name, Orsini, comes from the Latin *Ursus* which means *Bear*, you know the big furry animal, and my title as a Catholic priest is Father. Now Father in Italian translates familiarly into *Papa*; thus Papa Bear (no relation to Goldilocks).

This is an attempt to be an honest-to-goodness cookbook with many fine recipes, but as you will see, I have tried to make it a little something more. I hope you will laugh at my attempts to be humorous; ponder my attempts to be profound; and enjoy this wonderful life that God has given us while eating some of the best food this side of heaven.

Italian cooking has great simplicity, considerable originality and flexibility. You can enjoy inexpensive dishes or, with some prices today, take out a bank loan to make the more elegant dishes.

Italian housewives, many with large families and limited means, have for generations concentrated on making the best use of fresh local produce. The result is a tradition of practical dishes with distinctive flavors. Herbs, cheese, olive oil, tomatoes, and vegetables are used generously because they are readily available. It is from homespun recipes that the fabric of traditional Italian cooking has been woven.

The hallmarks of Italian cooking are simplicity, quality of ingredients and freshness of flavor. A restaurant serving overcooked lukewarm spaghetti or pizza smothered in a heavy blanket of reheated sauce does *not* represent the best of Italian cooking.

Italian cooking has strong regional character because only a hundred years ago Italy was a collection of individual States each with its own people, customs, traditions and foods. What is represented here in this book, for the most part, is the style of Southern Italy.

It should be noted that the flavor of Parmesan cheese is much finer, and the cost much less when it is bought by the chunk and freshly grated. Good Italian cooks are very particular about the use of *freshly* grated cheese with soups, pasta and rice.

Most of the ingredients in these recipes are available at local supermarkets; a few will have to be purchased from Italian specialty shops. Except where noted, all recipes will produce enough for four or five people.

Papa Bear's Favorite Italian Dishes

Chapter 1

Stop Off in Spain

I am convinced that Jesus loves me, "warts and all," because through a series of remarkable (at least to me) happenings which I recounted in my first book, *Hear My Confession*, He brought me to a personal experience of His living reality. With my second book, *The Anvil*, I tried to show that His love sometimes hurts, as all true love does. Both books sold surprisingly well and, as a result, I've made a lot of friends I might otherwise never have known. From them I've learned that God hasn't been tampering with me alone. In fact I learned that He is renewing the face of the earth. I also believe that, because if He could renew me, hard-head that I am, He is able to renew anyone or anything.

When I wrote my first two books, I tried to recall certain individuals who had a lasting influence in my life. Of course, when you start to name people, there's always the chance that you'll unintentionally leave someone out. I remember vividly that when these books hit the bookstores, not a few of my friends and relatives asked with a hopeful gleam in their eyes, "Hey Joe, is *my* name in your book?" My brother-in-law Joe

Varela was one who wanted to ask that question, but was too humble to do so. One night recently in pleasant conversation over good coffee and fattening doughnuts at his house we were discussing my writing this book. I told my brother-in-law that, although all of the recipes would be Italian, I would include two of his which would be Spanish. My brother-in-law is a warm and earnest Christian and I love him more as a blood brother than as merely an in-law. So to honor him and his Spanish heritage, we begin our fantastic culinary journey with two of his great native dishes. (I must confess however that I tampered a bit with some of the ingredients, so if they taste a little Italian, blame me.)

MEATBALLS ALLA SPAGNOLA

> 2 pounds chopped chuck
> 1 large onion, chopped
> 1 teaspoon salt
> ½ teaspoon black pepper
> 1 cup plain breadcrumbs
> 3 cloves garlic diced fine or 1 teaspoon garlic powder
> 1 green pepper chopped fine
> 1 egg

Mix and form meatballs. Fry till brown and set aside.

> ### Sauce:
>
> 1 onion, chopped
> 2 cloves garlic or ¾ teaspoon garlic powder
> 1 cup hot water in which is dissolved enough flour to make runny paste
> ½ teaspoon salt, pepper and paprika to taste

In same fry pan add 1 tablespoon oil. Sauté onions and garlic, add flour mixture and seasonings, simmer and stir for 10 minutes. Add meatballs and two quartered peeled potatoes, cover and simmer over low heat till potatoes are done.

CHICKEN ALLA SPAGNOLA

1 large frying chicken, quartered
¼ cup olive oil
1 onion, chopped
4 potatoes, peeled and quartered
3 green peppers, diced
2 minced garlic cloves
1 teaspoon salt
½ teaspoon black pepper

Dust chicken pieces with black pepper and brown on both sides in fry pan in hot oil. Remove chicken and set aside. Then sauté the onion, potatoes, green peppers, garlic cloves, salt and pepper in the same fry pan. Add all the browned chicken pieces with a pinch of saffron and simmer covered over low heat till potatoes and chicken are done.

Chapter 2

Let's Get Started

Antipasto, meaning "before the meal," is the first course of an Italian meal. Since Italian-Americans are becoming these days as weight-conscious as the rest of our society and there is a trend towards lighter meals and less starchy foods, an antipasto is often served instead of pasta. The antipasto can be extremely simple or as elaborate as you like, anything from a crisp tomato salad to a dozen different ingredients artistically combined like Insalata Suprema. The important point to remember is that the antipasto should complement the rest of the meal. What follows is a recipe for vegetable fritters Northern Italian style, a great beginning for any meal.

FRITTO MISTO DI VERDURE

1. *Cauliflower* 2. *Broccoli* 3. *Fennel* 4. *Celery*	*Parboiled i.e. boiled for a few minutes until tender crisp*
5. *Beets* 6. *Potatoes*	*These should be boiled thoroughly*
7. *Mushrooms* 8. *Eggplant* 9. *Zucchini squash* 10. *Tomatoes* 11. *Onions*	*Sliced raw and thin*

Coat the vegetables with frying batter and fry crisp and golden in olive oil. Drain on absorbent paper and serve immediately.

Recipe for Frying Batter

½ *cup flour*
½ *teaspoon salt*
2 *tablespoons olive oil*
⅝ *cup warm water*
1 *white of one large egg*

Sift the flour and salt into a bowl. Stir in the oil and water, forming a smooth fairly stiff batter. Beat well and let stand in refrigerator for 1 hour. Just before using, whisk the egg white to a light foam and fold gently into the batter.

MOZZARELLA IN CARROZZA
(Italian Fried Cheese Sandwich)

1½ ounce slice mozzarella (pizza cheese) for each sandwich
2 square slices firm bread for each sandwich
Flour
1 egg for each sandwich
Dash salt
Oil for frying

Remove crusts from bread. Sandwich the sliced cheese between the slices of bread and cut into halves or quarters. Dip in flour, then into lightly beaten and salted egg, leaving long enough for the bread to soak up the egg. Turn once. Drain, press sandwich firmly together and fry in hot oil until golden on both sides. Serve immediately. Makes a great lunch or hot antipasto.

Chapter 3

Italian Tomato Sauce Doesn't Come in a Can

The most important feature of Italian-American cooking is the indispensable tomato sauce. Without a tomato sauce correctly spiced, most Italian recipes that demand tomato sauce will taste like bland gruel prepared for patients with severe digestive problems. The secret is in the sauce. In my haphazard career as an amateur cook I've found that if you've spoiled the sauce then it's better to throw the whole thing away and start all over again.

One Saturday afternoon in July of 1972 as I was placing the finishing touches on a huge pot of tomato sauce that I was preparing in the rectory kitchen, Monsignor Mike Argullo, my pastor, joined me in the kitchen for the critical taste test, a spoonful of sauce on a hunk of Italian bread. A smile of delight crossed our faces and he exclaimed; "Now that's tomato sauce!"

Our housekeeper didn't work on Saturdays and Sundays, so I volunteered to prepare our meal for Saturday nights. Each

Saturday Monsignor Mike would watch as I cooked the meal and we would wait together for the three priests who joined us on weekends, Father Joe Narciso, Father Patrizio and Father Dooley, before we sat down to eat. While waiting that Saturday afternoon, I was telling Monsignor about the first time I tried to cook tomato sauce for two wonderful friends I hadn't seen in seven years, Joe Cassano and his wife Val. Just at that moment the telephone rang, I answered, and a voice asked:

"Is there a Father Orsini assigned there?"

"Yes," I answered suspiciously.

"Father Orsini who graduated from Seton Hall?"

"Yes."

"Is this he?"

"Yes."

"Where have you been Jo-Jo!"

I knew then it was Joe Cassano, my old college buddy. It was almost an unbelievable coincidence. He told me he had recently moved to South Jersey from Brooklyn, had added five more children to his family since I had visited him seven years ago on the occasion of the birth of his first child, and wanted me to visit him, Valerie and the children as soon as possible. After all those years, the Lord had led him to find me and rekindle a long neglected friendship. The Lord works in wonderful and mysterious ways. Now we can share, dear reader, the magic and mystery of my Mamma's famous tomato sauce.

MAMMA BEAR'S BASIC TOMATO SAUCE

2 large cans Italian plum tomatoes (2½ pound cans)
2 small cans of tomato paste
1½ cups water
2 large peeled thinly sliced onions
5 cloves finely minced garlic or 1 tablespoon garlic powder
1 teaspoon oregano
1 teaspoon sweet basil
1½ tablespoons salt
1 teaspoon pepper
1 tablespoon sugar
⅓ cup olive oil

Run tomatoes through food mill or chop in blender for a few seconds and reserve.

In large saucepan, sauté onions and garlic in olive oil till soft. Add salt, pepper, oregano, basil and stir. Add tomato paste and water, bring to simmer for 10 minutes. Add milled or blended peeled tomatoes, and sugar. Bring to slow boil, then simmer over low heat for 2½ to 3 hours, stirring occasionally. This sauce may be used for any pasta or rice dish that calls for tomato sauce.

VARIATIONS: You may add browned sausage, meatballs, chunks of beef, chicken pieces or pork chunks in any combination for the last hour of cooking in sauce. These meats are served along with the pasta for complete hearty meal.

SALSA PIZZAIOLA

The recipe for this distinctive sauce is Neapolitan in origin, and may be used to make pizza, steak pizzaiola, or spaghetti.

2 cloves garlic, peeled
1 pound ripe tomatoes (or 1 pound can peeled tomatoes)
2 tablespoons olive oil

> 1 teaspoon salt
> ½ teaspoon pepper
> 1 teaspoon oregano
> 1 teaspoon chopped parsley

Crush the garlic and skin the tomatoes. Put the oil and crushed garlic into a sauce pan and cook over a low heat for several minutes. Chop skinned tomatoes into fairly large pieces and add to pan with salt and pepper. Cook briskly for 5 minutes, until the ingredients have softened. Stir in oregano and parsley and use as desired.

Sometimes people avoid the above dishes because they find that tomato sauce is hard on their digestive systems. There is a solution for these unfortunate people in the next recipe from Northern Italy. With this easy to prepare sauce they can have their pasta and eat it too!

BECHAMEL SAUCE
(White Sauce for Macaroni)

From the northern regions of Italy comes this smooth and creamy sauce. This can be enhanced by adding grated cheddar or Parmesan cheese or a fistful of freshly chopped parsley.

> 4 tablespoons butter
> ¼ cup flour
> 2½ cups milk (boiling hot)
> Salt and pepper to taste

In a small saucepan melt the butter over gentle heat. Add the flour, and, using a wooden spoon, stir and cook without browning for several minutes. Remove from heat, and stir in the milk, little by little, mixing to a smooth sauce. Stir until boiling and simmer for 10 minutes. Season to taste with salt and pepper (a little nutmeg wouldn't hurt either).

Chapter 4

Pasta with Anything

For the Southern Italian, pasta (macaroni products), rather than bread, is the staff of life. Pasta goes with just about anything, meat, fish or vegetables. Pasta all by itself is a good source of protein as well as belly-filling carbohydrates. Pasta is to the Italian what the potato is to the Irishman.

A word of warning is needed for the calorie counter. Too much pasta means "full figures." But even the various weight watching organizations have recognized that one must feed his soul as well as slim down his body, and now allow a cup-full of the original "soul food," PASTA! Be careful now! These next recipes may wreck your resolve to look like Twiggy. But cheat a little and ENJOY!

There is a custom in many Italian-American families of making fresh pasta to go along with the fresh sauces. It takes a little more work and time, but the results are well worth the effort.

Try the following recipes for yourself and then you can

decide whether you will take the time or run down to your local store and depend upon the commercial products.

BASIC PASTA
(Homemade Macaroni)

> * *1 cup plain flour*
> *2 large eggs*
> *A little cold water*

To make pasta is really very simple once you have done it a few times and know the "feel" of it.

Sift the flour into a mound on a working surface and make a hole in the center. Crack the eggs into the hole and with the fingertips mix the yolks and the whites and then start drawing in the flour a little at a time. Add a very little cold water as necessary and continue mixing until a very firm but elastic dough is formed. Using the palm of your hand, knead the dough strongly for about ten minutes until smooth and silky, dusting with flour now and then to prevent sticking. Now with a rolling pin, roll out the dough first in one direction, then in the other, until the pasta is so thin that the graining of your surface can just be seen through it. It takes patience and a strong arm but this quantity should roll out to about 2 feet × 2 feet. Drape a clean cloth over the back of a kitchen chair and hang the pasta to dry for about 20 to 30 minutes, not longer. Then cut into desired shapes and lengths.

For Fettucine**

Roll the sheet of pasta up loosely and with a sharp knife cut across into ¼ inch strips. Unwind and hang the ribbons over

---

* You can increase the amounts of the ingredients proportionately to make more pasta as you need it.

** These are excellent to use with the Carbonara sauce (page 21).

back of chair to dry, then drop in boiling salted water until they rise to the surface.

For Lasagna

Cut the pasta into large enough rectangles or squares to fit your baking dish or pan and dry flat. Then proceed with the recipe for lasagna on page 15. You must of course cook the squares first in boiling salted water until they rise to the surface.

For Ravioli

After sheet has dried according to instructions given above, divide in half and roll into tissue thin pieces each about 12 inch square. Trim the edges.

Now prepare the filling. There are many different fillings for ravioli but this light cheese filling is simple and delicious.

Filling for Ravioli:

8 ounces ricotta (Italian pot cheese)
1 large egg
2 heaping teaspoons grated Parmesan cheese
Salt and pepper to taste
Sprinkling of chopped fresh parsley

Mix all ingredients together.

Lay one sheet of pasta flat on a working surface and with the side of a ruler lightly impress the dough to make it into 1½ inch squares (you can make them as small or as large as you wish). Put one small teaspoon of filling in the center of each square and with a small brush damp with water along the dividing marks in each direction (to help the edges stick firmly when the pasta is cut). Lay the second sheet of pasta lightly over the top and press together firmly along the marks in each direction. With a fluted edged cutter, or a sharp knife, cut along the marks and divide the ravioli into separate squares.

Cover with a floured cloth until ready to cook. Bring a large saucepan of water to a boil, lower the ravioli one by one gently into the water cooking in batches of fours to avoid overcrowding. As the ravioli rise to the top, give them another minute then remove with a perforated spoon. Serve very hot with generous covering of Mamma Bear's basic tomato sauce (p. 9).

Another favorite is the next recipe for

POTATO GNOCCHI

1 pound of potatoes, mashed
¾ cup regular flour
1 egg
1 tablespoon grated Parmesan cheese
Salt and pepper to taste

Mix together all ingredients thoroughly, forming a dough.

Roll into 1 inch finger shapes with your hands. Drop a few gnocchi at a time into boiling salted water and cook till they rise to the surface. Remove with a perforated spoon. Serve hot with Mamma Bear's basic tomato sauce (p. 9).

I have traveled by air to Italy seven times in the last ten years with Alitalia, the Italian Airlines. Almost every time I was served a delicious dish of cannelloni. I think it was the cannelloni that prompted me to use the same airlines time after time. So you won't have to take a trip to Italy just to taste them, I include my recipe for them.

CANNELLONI

Prepare one recipe for basic pasta (p. 12) and cut with a sharp knife into 4 squares. Cook in boiling salted water until they rise to the surface. Remove and cool. Then fill generously with the cheese filling given for ravioli on page 13. Roll the pasta carefully around the filling and make a stove pipe with each. Arrange side by side in a shallow oven dish and sprinkle with grated Parmesan cheese. Cover with tomato sauce (p. 9) and bake in 350° oven for 15 to 20 minutes.

FILLING VARIATIONS FOR CANNELLONI OR RAVIOLI

Ham Filling

6 ounces minced cooked ham
2 tablespoons melted butter
¼ cup chopped parsley
2 ounces grated cheese
1 beaten egg
2 slices bread
4 tablespoons milk
Salt and pepper

Fry the ham in melted butter. Soak the bread in the milk, and add it, the parsley, cheese, egg, salt and pepper to the ham. Mix well and fill pasta.

Spinach and Cheese Filling

5 ounce carton frozen chopped spinach
8 ounces ricotta or pot cheese
1 ounce grated Parmesan cheese
1 egg
Salt and pepper to taste

Allow the spinach to defrost, drain and squeeze very dry. Mix thoroughly with the remaining ingredients and add salt and pepper to taste. Now fill the pasta and cook as directed.

One of the reasons that you don't ,find too many skinny Italians is because they love to eat dishes like the following:

STUFFED SHELLS OR MANICOTTI

When in the supermarket, select either *large* shell macaroni or manicotti. Cook them to the directions on the package and then fill by spoon with the following:

Cheese Filling

2 *pounds ricotta (Italian pot cheese)*
2 *eggs*
½ *cup grated Parmesan cheese*
1 *cup mozzarella (pizza cheese)*
¼ *cup chopped parsley*
Salt and pepper to taste

Mix all ingredients together until smooth.
Once the macaroni has been stuffed, cover generously with basic tomato sauce (p. 9) and pop into 350° oven for ½ hour. Serve immediately.

LASAGNA

(A generous serving of this popular Italian dish is a meal in itself. It is best appreciated if you starve yourself for a day before sitting down to its delectable aroma and deliciously fattening rich taste.)

> *1 pound lasagna macaroni*
> *One recipe basic tomato sauce (p. 9)*
> *One recipe Mamma's meatballs (p. 56)*
> *1 pound sweet or hot Italian sausage*
> *One recipe cheese filling (p. 16)*

Cook the lasagna macaroni according to the directions on the package. Brown the Italian sausage, remove it from the skin and crumble it for easy use. Cover the bottom of a large pan with basic tomato sauce in which has been cooked the previously browned meatballs and sausage. Then cover with strips of cooked lasagna. On top of the lasagna arrange a generous covering of the following:

1. Cheese filling
2. Crumbled sausage and meatballs
3. Covering of tomato sauce

Then, cover this layer with an arrangement of cooked lasagna macaroni and follow same procedure as for the first layer. Make as many layers as your ingredients allow, but make sure you have enough lasagna macaroni to cover the top. Place in 350° oven for ½ hour. Remove and let it set for ½ hour. Then remove the topping of lasagna macaroni which will have become dried and crisp from the heat of the oven. Discard this, and then slice into generous servings. Over each serving pour a piping hot cover of tomato sauce that you have reserved. When you taste it, you will know why it is so popular.

TIMBALLO ALLA CALABRESE
(Macaroni Pie)

For the Crust:

2 cups all-purpose flour
7 tablespoons butter
¼ cup sugar

For the Filling:

¼ pound chicken giblets, diced (optional)
½ pound ground chuck
2 cups boiled mushrooms, diced
¼ cup dry white wine
2 cups basic tomato sauce (p. 9)
1 cup Bechamel sauce (p. 10)
1 pound cooked macaroni (ziti or mezzani)
1 cup grated Parmesan cheese
Pinch salt
2 egg yolks beaten with 3 tablespoons water

Preparation of crust: Grease a round, deep oven-proof dish and sprinkle it with a little flour. Combine ingredients for crust, mix well, and let stand for one hour. Roll it out ¼ inch thick and line the dish; reserve the rest of crust for the top.

Preparation of filling: Wash chicken giblets well. Dice. Heat 1 tablespoon butter in large saucepan. Brown giblets and ground meat lightly, stirring with fork to crumble the chopped meat. Add salt and wine. Let wine evaporate almost completely, then add the tomato sauce and diced mushrooms. Cover and simmer slowly for ½ hour. Meanwhile, toss the cooked macaroni (still hot), with the remaining butter, Parmesan cheese, and Bechamel sauce. Finally toss with tomato-meat sauce. Put the mixture into crust-lined dish, cover with remaining crust. Prick with fork. Bake in 450° oven for 20 minutes. You won't want to stop eating.

SPAGHETTI ALLA VONGOLE
(Clams and Spaghetti)

> *1 dozen small clams, scrubbed*
> *¾ cup olive oil*
> *2 cloves garlic, finely minced*
> *1¼ pounds peeled fresh tomatoes or two cups basic tomato sauce (p. 9)*
> *Salt and pepper to taste*
> *¼ cup chopped parsley*
> *1 pound spaghetti*

Put the clams in a saucepan with ¼ cup oil and heat. When the clams open, remove them from the heat and quickly detach the meat from the shells with a fork. Reserve the meat. Strain the stock in the saucepan through a fine sieve and set it aside. Sauté the garlic in the saucepan with the remaining oil until golden brown. Add tomatoes or sauce to the oil, season with salt and pepper and simmer until thickened. Add the clams and strained stock. Simmer briefly to warm through, mix in parsley. Serve the clam sauce over freshly cooked spaghetti.

SPAGHETTI ALLA QUARESIMA
(Lenten Spaghetti)

> *1 recipe for basic tomato sauce (p. 9)*
> *20 pitted black olives, quartered*
> *1 7 ounce can tuna packed in olive oil, flaked*
> *2 teaspoons capers, washed and drained (optional)*
> *1 pound spaghetti, linguini, or vermicelli*

Follow the recipe for basic tomato sauce (p. 9). Add olives, flaked tuna, and capers during last ½ hour of cooking. Serve over cooked spaghetti. This dish will delight and surprise your hungry family.

In my mother's home we have the following dishes once in a while as a pleasant change from macaroni with tomato sauce. The first one, I'm pretty sure, was taught to my Mom by my sister's godmother, Comare Raggio. Comare Raggio was a wonderful woman who was born in Sardinia, married her husband Carlo who had come from Genoa, and settled in New York. My parents were befriended by them when they arrived in New York from Italy, and when my sister Evelyn was born, Comare and Compare Raggio became her godparents. It is in their memory that I have included this recipe.

SPAGHETTI ALLA GENOVESE
(Spaghetti with Veal)

> 2 *pounds stewing veal*
> 1 *large onion, thinly sliced*
> 2 *cups water*
> ¼ *cup olive oil*
> ¼ *cup chopped parsley*
> 3 *large potatoes, peeled and quartered*
> 1 *tablespoon salt*
> 1 *teaspoon pepper*

In large saucepan, brown veal well in olive oil, then remove, then brown potatoes, add more oil if needed. Sauté onions in same pot, add salt, pepper and parsley. Then add cooked meat and potatoes. Simmer together for 5 minutes, add water, bring to boil over medium heat, then simmer over low heat for 1 hour. Serve with freshly cooked spaghetti.

AGLI'E OLIO
(Garlic, Oil and Cooked Spaghetti)

½ *cup olive oil*
8 *cloves garlic, peeled and whole*
1 *teaspoon salt*
½ *teaspoon pepper*
1 *pound cooked spaghetti*
2 *teaspoons chopped parsley*

Sauté garlic, parsley, salt and pepper over medium heat. When garlic begins to turn brown, remove from heat. Toss entire contents with 1 pound cooked spaghetti. Serve with a sprinkle of Italian breadcrumbs (p. 35).

SPAGHETTI ALLA CARBONARA

This is the only dish Mamma doesn't make, but I include it because I fell in love with it on my visit to Rome.

½ *pound bacon*
¼ *pound butter*
6 *eggs*
1 *cup light cream*
½ *cup grated Parmesan cheese*
Salt and pepper to taste
1 *pound cooked fettucine or linguini or spaghetti*

Cut the bacon into small pieces and sauté in butter in large skillet.

Beat the eggs lightly with cream and add cheese, salt and pepper.

Pour the mixture into the bacon in pan and stir gently, as for scrambled eggs, but do not allow mixture to set. (It should be wet.)

Pour over hot macaroni and toss. Sprinkle with grated Parmesan and serve immediately.

Chapter 5

Pasta with Everything

Fridays have always been special days for me since I was ordained. On Fridays after teaching school, I have always taken the trek up the New Jersey Turnpike to see my Mom and family for a few hours. On Saturday mornings the rides back down to South Jersey have always been made more pleasant because of my brief Friday evening visits home with the warm memories of solid family love *and* the taste of the next recipe still on my tongue.

Almost every Friday I arrive home to the warm embraces and kisses that my Mom showers on me just before my brother John's daily visit to her. My brother John's daily visits usually last about ten minutes, but on Friday he stays about a half hour. I have never figured out why he stays longer on Fridays. Either it's because I'm there or because he waits for Mamma's Friday question: "Vuoi 'nu piattu di fagioli, Gianni?" ("Would you like a dish of beans, John?") John smiles and says: "Yeah, Ma!" I love to watch him dipping a piece of Italian bread into his dish and wiping it clean.

Then follows the wait for my brother Oreste to arrive home before we sit down to supper. After about five minutes into the meal, the back door opens and in steps our regular Friday night visitor, my brother Toto (Anthony). My brother Oreste and I join in a chant: "Ma, U bordante è cca!" ("Ma, the boarder is here!") Mom smiles, hurries to fill a dish while saying: "Toto, figliu bellu, giust'a tempu, ancora c'è'." ("Toto, beautiful son, just in time, there's still some left.") Toto joins us in the wonderful sharing of family love and Mamma's pasta e fagioli. A little later, my brothers Mimi and Leo show up, and strangely enough there's always enough for them too. Finally brother John returns and the last of it is gone.

PASTA E FAGIOLI
(Macaroni and Beans—the Famous Pastafazool!)

> *Package of dry pinto beans or cranberry beans*
> *5 whole peeled cloves of garlic*
> *¼ cup olive oil*
> *1½ teaspoon salt*
> *1 teaspoon ground black pepper*
> *1 teaspoon tomato paste (optional)*
> *2 small peeled diced potatoes*

Soak the beans overnight in warm water. Drain and wash them. Place in large saucepan and cover with warm water. Bring to a boil over medium heat and then add the rest of the ingredients. Then simmer over low heat for 1 hour.

Serve mixed with 1 pound of cooked macaroni, such as ditali or ditalini, or cooked rice.

There is a story told about the main ingredient of this next recipe, chickpeas or Ceci. When Sicily was held by France, the Sicilians were terribly abused by their French masters. Finally the proud Sicilians couldn't take anymore and began a bloody, ultimately successful revolt, and rid their island of the hated French. In fact some historians report that the infamous

Mafia was formed at this time as a part of this revolt against foreign oppression. They say that the word Mafia is an abbreviation of the following war cry: *M*orte *A*lla *F*rancia *I*talia *A*nnella! (Death to France Italy Cries). In the cleanup operation that followed this Sicilian revolt, bands of Sicilian patriots would confront suspected Frenchmen with a handful of chickpeas pronounced in the Sicilian dialect "Ciceri" (Chicheri) and ask: "Quisti chi sunu?" (What are these?) The Frenchmen had mastered the Sicilian dialect except the distinctive "chi" sound in the word "ciceri." They would pronounce the sound as "ki." If they did, they were executed on the spot. As with many stories in Italian tradition we really don't know if they are true or not, so we say "Se non è vero, è ben trovato." (If it's not true, it's still a good story.) We hope this rather gruesome story doesn't prevent you from enjoying this excellent dish.

PASTA E CECI
(Macaroni and Chickpeas)

> *2 cans of chickpeas (garabanzos)*
> *2 cloves finely minced garlic*
> *¼ cup olive oil*
> *½ cup chopped parsley*
> *Salt and pepper to taste*
> *1 pound cooked macaroni (ditali or ditalini)*

Sauté the garlic in the olive oil, and then add the two cans of chickpeas. Add the chopped parsley and salt and pepper to taste. Simmer over low heat for ½ hour, and serve with cooked macaroni.

FAGGIOLINI CON SPAGHETTI
(Pasta with Vegetables)

> 1 *pound fresh string beans, whole*
> 2 *cloves garlic, finely minced*
> 2 *tablespoons olive oil*
> 2 *medium size potatoes, diced*
> 2 *cups water*
> 1 *tablespoon salt*
> ½ *teaspoon black pepper*
> 1 *pound cooked spaghetti*

In a large saucepan, sauté garlic in the oil. Add stringbeans. Stir and simmer for five minutes. Add the water, potatoes, salt and pepper. Bring to a boil, then simmer on low heat for 1 hour. Mix with cooked spaghetti and serve.

PASTA E CAVOLIAFIORE
(Cauliflower)

> 1 *large head cauliflower broken into bite-sized pieces*
> 3 *cloves minced garlic*
> ¼ *cup olive oil*
> 1 *cup crushed tomatoes*
> ½ *teaspoon crushed red pepper*
> 1 *tablespoon salt*
> *Dash of black pepper*
> 1 *pound cooked macaroni (ziti or rigatoni)*

In a large saucepan sauté the garlic in oil. Add the tomatoes and red pepper. Bring to an easy boil and add cauliflower, salt and pepper. Simmer for an hour, adding just enough water to cover cauliflower.

Serve mixed with the macaroni.

BROCCOLI E PASTA
(Broccoli with Spaghetti)

> *1 or 2 fresh bunches of broccoli*
> *3 cloves garlic, finely minced*
> *¼ cup olive oil*
> *1 cup water*
> *1 teaspoon crushed red pepper*
> *1½ teaspoons salt*

Wash broccoli carefully and cut off the tough stalks.

In large saucepan sauté garlic in the oil. Add the water. Bring to an easy boil and add broccoli, salt and red pepper. Simmer for 1 hour or until broccoli is fork tender, adding water if needed.

Serve as a vegetable or mix with 1 pound of cooked spaghetti.

If you like broccoli, this will become one of your favorite dishes.

ZITI ALLA SICILIANA
(Baked Macaroni—Sicilian Style)

> *1 pound ziti or mezzani macaroni*
> *1 large eggplant*
> *1 pound mozzarella (pizza cheese) grated*
> *3 cups basic tomato sauce (p. 9)*
> *1 cup grated Parmesan cheese*

Cook the macaroni. Slice the eggplant into thin slices and sauté in skillet till soft in ¼ cup olive oil. Cover the bottom of an ovenproof pan with one cup of the sauce, followed by a layer of macaroni, then grated mozzarella, then cooked eggplant sprinkled with Parmesan, then more sauce. Repeat layers, covering top with remainder of sauce. Cook in 350° oven for ½ hour. Serve immediately.

SPAGHETTI CON SALSA VERDE
(Spaghetti with Green Sauce)

1 clove garlic, finely chopped
1 tablespoon pine nuts, finely chopped
2 cups freshly washed basil leaves
½ teaspoon salt
1 cup grated Parmesan cheese
1 pinch cayenne pepper
1 cup olive oil
¼ cup boiling chicken stock

In an electric blender, combine half the olive oil with the rest of the ingredients and blend on low speed until they have reached the consistency of a paste. Continue blending on low speed, adding the remainder of the oil gradually.

Pour this green sauce over freshly cooked spaghetti or fettucine. This would be a terrific dish to serve on St. Patrick's Day.

SPAGHETTI CON SALSA DI FUNGHI
(Spaghetti with Mushroom Sauce)

2 cups of basic tomato sauce (p. 9)
1 pound fresh small mushrooms
¼ cup grated Parmesan cheese
½ cup dry white wine
3 tablespoons butter

Wash the mushrooms well and drain to dry. Parboil the mushrooms in boiling salted water for 10 minutes. Drain. In a large saucepan, sauté the mushrooms in the butter until turning light brown. Add the cheese and stir. Add the wine and simmer briskly until the wine evaporates. Add the tomato sauce and simmer until heated through. Pour over freshly cooked spaghetti or linguini.

SPAGHETTI ALLA GIARDINIERA
(Spaghetti Gardener's Style)

2 green peppers, cut into strips
1 onion, chopped
1 clove garlic, minced
7 tablespoons butter
½ cup olive oil
1 ten ounce package frozen artichoke hearts, defrosted
½ pound button mushrooms, sliced
½ pound lima beans, shelled
1 pound green peas, shelled
1 teaspoon salt
½ teaspoon black pepper
½ cup dry red wine
1 pound tomatoes peeled or 1½ cups basic tomato sauce (p. 9)
1 pound spaghetti
¾ cup grated Parmesan cheese

Sauté onion and garlic until golden brown in a large saucepan with butter and oil. Add peppers, artichoke hearts, mushrooms, beans and peas. Season with salt and pepper and add the wine. When wine has partially evaporated add tomatoes or tomato sauce. Cover the pan and simmer for ½ hour. Pour over cooked spaghetti and top with cheese. A vegetarian's delight!

FETTUCINE VERDI AI QUATTRO STAGIONI
(Pasta—Four Seasons Style)

¼ pound Swiss cheese, cubed
¼ pound muenster cheese, cubed
¼ pound mozzarella cheese, cubed
1 cup heated milk
⅓ cup melted butter
1 cup grated Parmesan cheese
1 pound green (spinach) noodles

Soak the cubed cheeses in the heated milk for one hour. The cheeses should soften but not melt. Cook the green noodles according to directions on package, drain, and turn into a hot, ovenproof casserole dish. Sprinkle with butter and add 3 tablespoons of the grated Parmesan. Pour half of the cheese sauce onto the noodles and toss gently. Pour remaining sauce over the top and garnish with a heavy sprinkling of grated Parmesan. Place in 450° oven for 10 minutes. Remove, sprinkle rest of Parmesan and serve. Protein rich and savory!

Chapter 6

A Nice Change from Pasta

RISOTTO
(Nice Rice)

Northern Italy is as well known for its rice casseroles and corn meal dishes as Southern Italy is for its pasta specialties. We give this fact a nod by the addition of the following dishes typical of the North but made tastier through Southern interpretation. I think you will find them a nice change from pasta.

In 1965 I was teaching Latin at Camden Catholic High School and as it happened I had as students two brothers, one a sophomore, the other a freshman, named Anthony and Steven Oswald. I quickly became good friends with their family and after a short while I invaded their kitchen. Norma (Campana) Oswald, the mom of the Oswald clan (8 children, 1 Mom, 1 Dad, and 2 cats), became my co-chef. We cooked and cooked and got heavier and heavier. One of our favorite dishes was a recipe I had gotten from an Italian Cistercian Monk, Father Giuliano Bruni. The following dish takes a lot of time and preparation but it is well worth the effort.

RISOTTO FRA GIULIANO
(Father Julian's Special Rice Casserole)

A. *1 large can (2½ pounds) Italian peeled tomatoes*
    3 cloves finely minced garlic
    2 medium onions, peeled and thinly sliced
    1 teaspoon salt
    ½ teaspoon pepper
    ½ teaspoon sugar
    ¼ cup olive oil
    1 pound fresh mushrooms, washed and chopped
    1 pound chopped meat (chuck)

Run the tomatoes quickly through a food-mill or chop them in a blender. In a large saucepan sauté garlic and onions until soft. Add mushrooms and sauté for about 10 minutes. Add spices and chopped meat (crumble into pan) and stir with fork until the meat is beginning to brown. Stir in crushed tomatoes, and simmer over low heat for 1 hour. Sauce should be very thick. Set aside.

B.   *2 cups rice*
      5 cups chicken stock (p. 48)

Boil the rice in the chicken stock. If you don't want to go
through the bother of making fresh chicken soup, you may use
chicken broth powder or cubes, or clear canned chicken broth.
Cook the rice until all the liquid is absorbed. Set aside.

C.   *1 pound mozzarella cheese, grated*
      ½ cup Parmesan, grated
      3 eggs
      Salt and pepper to taste.

Set aside the grated mozzarella. Beat well together eggs, grated
Parmesan, salt and pepper.
   You will need a well-greased tubular spring-pan. Take half
of the cooled cooked rice and mix with half of the grated
mozzarella. Pack this mixture into bottom half of the pan. Wet
with three tablespoons of the beaten egg mixture, press down
with spoon forming a trench in the middle of the packed rice.
Pour in meat and mushroom sauce, saving about ¼ cup. Add
rest of the rice and mozzarella. Pack down. Pour remainder of
egg mixture over rice. Top with rest of the sauce. Place in
375° oven for 45 minutes. Allow to cool for one hour, remove
sides of pan, cut in large wedges and serve.

RISOTTO CALABRESE
(Hearty Rice Main Dish)

   2 eight ounce cans of tomato sauce or 2 cups of basic tomato sauce
      (p. 9)
   1 large onion, finely sliced
   1 small clove garlic finely minced
   1 teaspoon salt
   1 teaspoon crushed red pepper
   2 peeled diced raw potatoes

4 cups cooked rice
⅛ cup olive oil

Sauté onion, garlic, salt and red pepper over low heat. Add tomato sauce and potatoes and simmer over low heat for 1 hour. Mix with cooked rice and serve hot sprinkled with grated Parmesan cheese.

From the sun-drenched island of Sicily, I must share a great recipe that should become a favorite in your home.

ARANCINI
(Sicilian Rice Balls)

1 cup basic tomato sauce (p. 9) or 1 small can tomato sauce
1 cup rice
3 ounces grated Parmesan cheese
2 small eggs
Salt to taste

Simmer the tomato sauce in an uncovered pan until of a thick consistency. Cook the rice in boiling salted water until tender, about 20 minutes. Drain thoroughly, add cheese, eggs, salt and a tablespoon of tomato sauce, mix well, and leave until cold.

Filling:

2 ounces mozzarella cheese
2 ounces salami or ham
Dash of salt and pepper
2 tablespoons thick tomato sauce

Shred the mozzarella, cut up the salami or ham into tiny pieces and mix together with the thick tomato sauce.

Take one large spoonful of the rice mixture in the palm of the hand, put 1 teaspoon of the filling in the center, place more rice mixture over the top and form into a ball the size of a small orange. Coat thoroughly with plain fine dry breadcrumbs, then fry in hot deep fat or oil until golden. Serve with a spoonful of tomato sauce.

POLENTA CALABRESE
(Corn Meal with a Zip)

> 2 *onions, thinly sliced*
> ¼ *cup olive oil*
> 1 *teaspoon crushed red pepper*
> 1 *tablespoon salt*
> 2 *eight ounce cans tomato sauce or 2 cups basic tomato sauce*
> ¾ *cup yellow corn meal*
> 2 *cups warm water*
> 2 *links Italian sausage*

Sauté onions in olive oil. Stir in pepper and salt. Add tomato sauce and simmer slowly in covered saucepot for ½ hour. Add 2 cups warm water and the cornmeal. Cook, stirring constantly for 30 minutes over low heat.

Add 2 links of Italian sausage, skinned and nicely browned. Crumble the meat and stir into cornmeal mixture.

Serve hot, topped with grated Parmesan cheese. Or allow to get cold and form into patties. Fry patties until golden brown in a little olive oil.

Chapter 7

A Crumb Is a Crumb!

ITALIAN BREADCRUMBS

You will notice that many of these recipes call for Italian breadcrumbs. You'll find they are tasty and can transform many simple items into culinary masterpieces.

Mix together:

- *1 pound dry breadcrumbs*
- *½ cup chopped parsley*
- *3 cloves finely minced garlic or 1 tablespoon garlic powder*
- *1½ teaspoons salt*
- *1 teaspoon pepper*
- *1 cup grated Parmesan cheese*

These basic breadcrumbs are used as coatings and stuffings in a variety of dishes such as the following:

1. Veal cutlets: Dip cutlets in slightly beaten egg, coat with Italian breadcrumbs and fry to golden brown in olive oil.

2. Tomato cutlets: Cut slightly green tomatoes into ¼ inch slices. Dip in slightly beaten egg, coat with Italian breadcrumbs and fry to golden brown in olive oil.

3. Pork chops: Dip in slightly beaten egg, coat with Italian breadcrumbs and fry to golden brown in olive oil.

4. Ricotta cutlets: Ricotta must be the dry type you can slice. Slice 1 inch thick. Dip in egg, breadcrumbs, and fry to brown in olive oil.

5. Eggplant cutlets: Wash, peel and cut eggplant into ¼ inch slices. Salt slices and place in collander to drain liquid for ½ hour. Pat slices dry, dip in lightly beaten egg, cover with breadcrumbs and fry in olive oil till golden brown.

In these days of economic inflation, most of us find it difficult to keep up with the rise in food prices. Though we are unwilling to cut down on the quality and quantity of food on our family tables, at the same time we don't want to wind up on welfare either. The next recipe is my own recent invention and may help us in our present situation.

INFLATION MEATLESS BALLS

1 recipe Italian breadcrumbs (p. 35)
1 pound grated mozzarella cheese
2 eggs

Mix all ingredients together well to form a rather thick mixture. If you find that when you try to roll spoonfuls of the mixture into balls that they will not hold together, add water until they do. Form into small balls with your hands and fry in hot oil until golden brown. They may be eaten as is, or served in tomato sauce.

STUFFED PEPPERS

You may make as many as you want and use either frying peppers or bell peppers. The frying peppers are cooked in a skillet in ¼ cup olive oil and the bell peppers are cooked in a pan in a 350° oven until tender.

Frying peppers: Wash, slice off tops, remove core and seeds. Stuff with Italian breadcrumbs (p. 35), and sauté in skillet until bottoms become soft. Then carefully turn over and sauté covered until tender. Serve hot or cold. Good also as an antipasto.

Bell peppers: Wash, slice off tops, remove core and seeds. Stuff with Italian breadcrumbs (p. 35), place in pan, drizzle with olive oil and bake in 350° oven till tender. Serve hot or cold.

STUFFED TOMATOES

Choose as many large ripe tomatoes as you wish. Wash, remove dark core, slice about ¼ inch off top, scoop out meat of tomato and seeds (save this to add to tomato sauce). Stuff tomatoes with Italian breadcrumbs (p. 35), drizzle with olive oil, place sliced tops back on tomatoes, place in pan. Bake in 350° oven until tender. Serve hot or cold. Good also as an antipasto.

STUFFED ARTICHOKES

Wash. Remove tough outer leaves and remove choke with apple corer. Turn artichokes upside down on flat surface and press down hard to open. Fill with spoon using Italian breadcrumbs (p. 35) to which chopped green or black olives have been added. Place stuffed artichokes in heavy pot, drizzle with olive oil and add enough water to cover bottoms of artichokes. Cover and simmer over low heat for about 1 hour until outer leaves can be easily torn off. You eat these by taking leaves in your hand, one at a time, and scrape against lower and upper teeth as you bite into them.

STUFFED MUSHROOMS

1 pound fresh mushrooms
Italian breadcrumbs
Olive oil

Wash mushrooms and boil for ½ hour. Drain and wash again in cold water. Remove stems and chop fine; add them to the breadcrumbs, and stuff the mushroom caps with the resulting mixture. Place stuffed caps in pan oiled with olive oil, drizzle with olive oil and bake at 350° for ½ hour. Serve hot.

Chapter 8

Vegetables Worth Eating

Many vegetables served in the American style are usually overcooked, bland and tasteless affairs served with a pat of butter. In fact if it weren't for Popeye, most kids wouldn't touch vegetables with a ten-foot pole. Italians, on the other hand, consume vegetables by the ton. I'm sure it's not because they're vitamin and mineral conscious, but because the way Italians prepare their vegetables tickles the palate. What follows are a few ways to make vegetables very popular to your family and guests.

GIAMBOTTO
(Vegetable Stew Featuring Zucchini)

> 5 *medium unpeeled zucchini squash, washed, ends sliced off and diced*
> 1 *medium eggplant, washed, peeled and diced*
> 2 *medium potatoes, washed, peeled and diced*
> 3 *cloves garlic, finely minced, or 1 teaspoon garlic powder*
> ½ *pound fresh string beans, washed and diced*
> 2 *cans tomato sauce or 2 cups freshly crushed tomatoes*
> 1 *medium onion, thinly sliced*
> ¼ *cup olive oil*
> 1 *tablespoon salt*
> 1 *tablespoon pepper or crushed red pepper*

In a large saucepan sauté in olive oil the onion and garlic. Then add the tomatoes or tomato sauce, potatoes, string beans, eggplant, salt and pepper and allow to simmer for one hour. Add the zucchini squash and allow to simmer for another ½ hour. Serve hot in soup bowls with buttered hot Italian bread.

POLPETTI DI MELANZANE
(Mamma's Own Original Mock Meatballs Made from Eggplant)

> 2 *large eggplants*
> 2 *cups Italian breadcrumbs*
> ¼ *cup chopped parsley*
> 3 *cloves finely minced garlic or 1 teaspoon garlic powder*
> 2 *eggs*
> 1½ *cups grated Parmesan cheese*

Wash eggplant and cut off ends, peel, then slice into quarters and boil in salted water until soft. Place in collander to drain and cool. Once cooled, remove most water from eggplant by carefully squeezing. Combine the eggplant with the remainder of the ingredients in a large mixing bowl. Mix well and add more breadcrumbs as needed until you can form mixture into 1 inch balls. Roll them in breadcrumbs and fry in olive oil until very brown. You can serve these as a vegetable side dish or drop them in our basic tomato sauce during the last fifteen minutes of cooking the sauce and serve as a meat substitute with spaghetti. May also be used as a hot antipasto.

EGGPLANT PARMIGIANA

Make eggplant cutlets (p. 36) from three large eggplants. In a baking dish or pan, cover bottom with tomato sauce (p. 9), then cover with eggplant cutlets. Cover with grated mozzarella cheese (pizza cheese), slice of hard-boiled egg, strips of Italian salami or mortadella, and generous sprinkle of grated Parmesan cheese, cover again with tomato sauce. In this way make as many layers as you want, making sure top layer is generously covered with tomato sauce. Bake in 350° oven for ½ hour. Let set for ½ hour and serve in large slices.

This is a good substitute for meat as eggplant is a rich source of protein. Served with a green salad and some crusty Italian bread. Molto buono! (Very good!)

ASPARAGUS AL PROSCIUTTO

4 slices Italian ham
1 pound cooked asparagus spears
1 tablespoon olive oil
½ cup grated Parmesan cheese
¼ cup chopped parsley

Frizzle ham in oil for 3 minutes. Then arrange ham slices in baking dish. Place equal number of asparagus spears on each slice. Sprinkle with cheese, dot with butter, place in 375° oven for 15 minutes. Serve hot garnished with parsley.

PANICOLO ITALIANO
(Italian Corn)

>6 tablespoons olive oil
>3 cloves finely chopped garlic
>12 ounce can whole kernel corn
>1 teaspoon sweet basil
>½ teaspoon salt
>½ teaspoon pepper
>⅓ cup grated Parmesan cheese
>¼ cup chopped parsley

Sauté garlic in oil, add drained corn and all ingredients except cheese. Toss well. Sprinkle with cheese, cook till cheese is melted and serve hot.

MINESTRA CALABRESE
(Vegetable Stew)

>2 large heads of escarole, washed thoroughly and torn in pieces
>2 celery stalks, washed and chopped
>1 pound fresh spinach, washed and torn into pieces
>1 small cabbage, cut into small pieces
>2 zucchini squash, unpeeled, washed and cut into small pieces
>1 large onion, thinly sliced
>2 cloves of garlic finely minced or 1 teaspoon garlic powder
>1 large tomato, peeled and quartered
>1 tablespoon salt
>1 teaspoon crushed red pepper
>¼ cup olive oil

In a large deep saucepan sauté the onion and garlic in oil. Add each vegetable, one kind at a time, and sauté until tender crisp. Add salt and red pepper and just enough water to cover. Simmer for one hour. You may add a can or two of white cannelini beans near the end of cooking time, and serve in bowls sprinkled with grated Parmesan cheese for a hearty and healthy dish.

FUNGHI ALLA CASA NOSTRA
(Tasty Fried Mushrooms)

1 pound fresh white mushrooms
1 cup all-purpose flour
1 teaspoon salt
½ teaspoon pepper
3 small finely minced garlic cloves or 1 teaspoon garlic powder
¼ cup olive oil

Boil the mushrooms in salted water for ½ hour. Drain, then dredge in 1 cup all purpose flour, seasoned with salt, pepper and garlic.
Fry until golden and toasty brown in ¼ cup olive oil.

I have one sister-in-law who is not of Italian descent, May, the wife of my brother Mimi (short for Dominick). I can remember that when they were courting and she was over my house for dinner, we always had to have boiled ham and mayonnaise on hand. We would all sit down to one of Mamma's masterpieces and poor May would timidly ask: "Could I have a ham sandwich?"

Over the years she has become Italian in taste by the process of absorption. Now from her kitchen wafts the soul-stirring aromas of garlic and grated Italian cheese. I don't think she's had a ham sandwich in years. I dedicate these next two recipes to her because when she tasted them, she insisted that Mamma teach her how to make them. As you'll see, they're a far cry from a meager ham sandwich.

CAPUCCIO E RISO
(Cabbage and Rice)

>   1　*large head of cabbage chopped*
>   1　*medium onion, thinly sliced*
>   1　*clove garlic, finely minced*
>   ¼　*cup olive oil*
>   1　*teaspoon salt*
>   1　*teaspoon crushed red pepper*

In large saucepan, sauté in oil the onion, garlic, salt and pepper. Add chopped cabbage and stir. Cover and simmer over low heat for 1 hour.

Combine with 1 cup of cooked rice and serve hot sprinkled lightly with grated Parmesan cheese.

CAPUCCIO ESTIVE
(Summer Cabbage)

>   2　*small fresh heads of cabbage, chopped coarsely*
>   1　*small clove garlic, minced*
>   2　*large fresh ripe tomatoes, peeled and crushed*
>   ¼　*cup olive oil*
>   1　*teaspoon salt*
>   ½　*teaspoon crushed red pepper*
>   2　*links Italian sausage, sliced or crumbled and browned*

In large saucepan, lightly sauté garlic in oil, add sausage and brown. Add tomatoes, simmer for 5 minutes. Add cabbage, salt and pepper. Cover and simmer over low heat for ½ hour stirring occasionally. Serve hot as main dish or a side dish with main course.

We have a beautiful family custom in my house. Every one of my brothers stops in every day to pay a visit to Mamma, even if it's only for ten minutes. When Mamma has a plateful of these delightful little delicacies on the table, my brothers usually stay a little longer. When you taste them you'll know why.

FRITTELLI CALABRESI

Basic Flour Paste:

1 cup flour
1 clove finely minced garlic
1 teaspoon salt
½ teaspoon pepper
1 teaspoon chopped parsley
Enough water to make thin paste

You may use this basic paste to fry golden brown in olive oil the following items:

1. Potatoes:
   Boil in skin. Cool. Peel and slice in ¼ inch slices. Dip in paste and fry.
2. Cauliflower:
   Boil flowerettes in salted water until tender. Cool Dip in paste and fry.
3. Zucchini and Pumpkin flowers:
   Wash carefully. Squeeze dry. Dip in paste and fry.
4. Mushrooms:
   Boil 5 minutes in salted water. Drain, add to paste and spoon into skillet. Fry till golden brown.
5. Beets:
   Boil in salted water until tender. Drain, slice in ¼ inch pieces, dip in paste and fry.

I'm sure you'll enjoy the next two recipes. I owe them to my sister-in-law, Marie, the wife of my brother, John, and the recent proud grandmother of twin boys.

PANZAROTTI
(Potato Croquettes)

> *5 large raw potatoes*
> *1½ cups Italian breadcrumbs*
> *¾ cup grated Parmesan cheese*
> *¼ cup chopped parsley*
> *3 cloves of finely minced garlic or 1½ teaspoons garlic powder*
> *¼ pound Italian salami, chopped*

Peel and quarter potatoes, then boil until soft in salted water. Allow to cool, then mash. Add the remaining ingredients to the mashed potatoes. Mix together well and form into oblong croquettes. Fry until golden brown in hot olive oil.

CALZONI
(Delightful Hot Appetizers)

> *2 cans refrigerated biscuits*
> *½ pound Italian salami or pepperoni, chopped*
> *½ pound grated mozzarella, Swiss or muenster cheese*
> *½ pound of grated Parmesan cheese*

Roll out biscuits and fill the center of each with a generous spoonful of a mixture of the remaining ingredients. Fold biscuits to center and pinch closed. Place each calzoni on an oiled cookie sheet pinched side down and bake in a 375° oven until very brown. Serve immediately.

Chapter 9

Zuppa!

Many biblical scholars say that the next dish was the "mess of pottage" for which Esau sold his birthright. When you taste it, you can hardly blame Esau. Mamma Orsini's own recipe for this dish has many times evoked the comment: "Questu piattu fa resuscitare i morti!," which means, "this dish would bring back the dead!" Of course we know that the dead will rise again, not due to this lentil soup, as delicious as it is, but because of the power of Jesus' Resurrection. Here it is now! This recipe alone is worth the price of this whole book . . . Presenting . . .

PAPA BEAR'S OWN LENTIL SOUP

1 pound dried lentils (wash them first)
2 medium onions, diced   1½ teaspoons salt
3 cloves garlic, minced   ½ teaspoon black pepper
2 freshly peeled tomatoes, quartered   1 teaspoon oregano
2 carrots, peeled and diced   ½ cup olive oil
2 potatoes, peeled and diced   2 quarts water

In large pot, bring water to boil. Add all ingredients at once, just throw them in together. Allow to boil for 15 minutes, then simmer on low heat for ½ hour. Cooked rice or macaroni may be added for a stick to the ribs dish. Nothing like it!

BRODO DI POLLO
(Mamma's Chicken Soup)

> 1 large whole soup or stewing chicken
> ½ cup chopped parsley
> 1 tablespoon salt

Wash chicken well. Place chicken in large pot and cover with water. Bring to a rolling boil, for about 5 minutes. Remove chicken, and discard water. Place chicken back in pot, add fresh water and bring to a slow boil. Add parsley and salt. Simmer for 1½ hours over low heat until chicken begins to fall apart.

Serve hot with cooked rice or soup macaroni and sprinkle with grated Parmesan cheese to taste.

For holidays as a first course this soup may be made special by the addition of marble-sized meatballs. (Use recipe on p. 56). One exception: don't fry these little meatballs, just drop them in the simmering soup.

There is nothing like a bowl of good hot soup to warm one's body and lift one's drooping spirits. The recipe given for chicken soup included the suggestion of adding tiny meatballs to make it more festive. If you were to travel south from Calabria you would reach the wonderful island of Sicily. Much has been written about Sicily and its sometimes mysterious people. Some may be true, but a lot of what you hear I believe is fantasy. I have found some Sicilians to be as warm and friendly as the island's gorgeous climate and others as fiery as the red hot peppers grown there. I may be partial to Sicily and Sicilians because my mother's father was born there, but I think if you try the following two recipes for Sicilian condiments for chicken soup, you will conclude that a people who can make something so delicious can't be as bad as others say.

I owe thanks for these two recipes to the grandmother of a Sicilian-American family, the Bottino family of Lindenwold, New Jersey, whose food and love I am privileged to share on many occasions.

SICILIAN SOUP CONDIMENTS

1. Scapelli:

2 eggs
½ teaspoon salt
Dash of black pepper
¼ cup grated Parmesan cheese
1 tablespoon all-purpose flour

Mix all above in a bowl and beat well, then gradually add enough all-purpose flour, a little at a time, to make an easy-to-pour batter (about the consistency of pancake batter).

Oil or grease lightly a large skillet and place over a high flame. Pour batter into skillet and cook as if a pancake. When bottom is turning brown, turn quickly, and brown other side. Remove from skillet, allow to cool, then roll tightly, and with a sharp knife, cut into narrow slices (⅛ inch).

Drop rolled slices into bottom of soup bowls, pour on piping hot chicken broth, sprinkle with grated Parmesan and serve.

2. *Quadrati d'Uova (Egg Squares)*

6 eggs
½ cup grated Parmesan cheese
1½ teaspoons salt
1 teaspoon black pepper
1 cup chopped parsley

Beat all ingredients together well, pour into well-oiled or greased shallow (½ to 1 inch) oven pan. Place in 350° oven approximately 15 minutes or until egg mixture is hard cooked (dry and firm). Remove and let get cold. Then cut into 1 inch squares. Drop generous amounts of these squares into bottom of soup bowls, pour on piping hot chicken broth, sprinkle with grated Parmesan and serve.

Another favorite of mine is the following recipe I tasted in Bologna, Italy. You begin by using the recipe for Mamma Bear's chicken soup (p. 48), and prepare the following:

PASSATELLI IN BRODO
(Cheese Noodles in Broth)

2½ cups chicken broth (p. 48)
1 egg
3 tablespoons grated Parmesan cheese
3 tablespoons fine plain breadcrumbs
2 level teaspoons flour
Piece of butter the size of a walnut

Bring the broth to a boil in a saucepan. Break the egg in a large bowl, add the cheese, breadcrumbs, flour, and butter. Work into a *stiff* paste with a wooden spoon, adding, if necessary, more breadcrumbs. Press the pasta through a coarse holed colander or mouli mill into the fast boiling soup. When the noodles rise to the surface, in 1-2 minutes, remove pot from the heat and let stand for 5 minutes before serving.

There is one more variation for satisfying bowls of soup that can easily be made the main course in these days of penny pinching. It comes from the medieval city of Pavia and features protein-rich eggs combined with filling toasted Italian bread.

ZUPPA PAVESE
(Soup from Pavia)

> 7 *cups chicken stock (p. 48)*
> 6 *large slices Italian bread*
> 2 *tablespoons butter*
> 6 *eggs*
> ½ *cup grated Parmesan cheese*

Melt butter over low heat in fry pan. Toast the slices of bread in the hot butter until golden brown. Place the slices in the center of ovenproof soup dishes and break an egg carefully over each slice of bread. Place the dishes in a 450° oven until the whites of the eggs set lightly. Remove from oven and pour hot chicken stock over the contents of the dishes to fill them. Sprinkle heavily with cheese, add a dash of freshly ground black pepper and serve immediately. Mmm . . . Mmm good!

Chapter 10

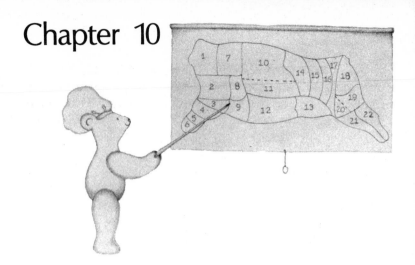

Meats Worth Their Price

My mother has a way with steak and roast beef that turns an ordinary piece of meat into an epicurean delight. She concocts a simple marinade in which she soaks the meat for about an hour and uses the marinade to baste while cooking. The resulting juices are served as a gravy with the meat to be sopped up with hefty chunks of Italian bread. Since the prices of beef today make it almost as valuable as gold, the marinade will make it taste as good as it costs.

When you use this recipe, please be sure that you use *all* the ingredients. I emphasize this because I have some very close friends in Pine Hill who didn't, and their supper turned out disastrously. These friends are Tony and Anne-Marie Ianucci. One day Anne-Marie bought some beautiful steak and decided that she would surprise her husband and kids by cooking the steak with the marinade she had heard me talk about. But she didn't remember the entire recipe. All she remembered was that I had said to use wine vinegar. Well, she did. About half a bottle. That night at dinner time she produced the steak, which looked great, and her family dug in enthusiastically. GAH! In no time at all, the whole family had the worst case of puckered lips in Pine Hill's history. After they had recovered slightly, they tossed the rest of the steak to their dog. The poor thing took one sniff and then ran into the dog house.

ITALIAN BEEF MARINADE

⅔ *cup olive oil*
¼ *cup red wine vinegar (here is the secret: the vinegar acts as a natural tenderizer!)*
1 *teaspoon oregano*
3 *cloves of finely minced garlic or 1 teaspoon garlic powder*
1 *teaspoon salt*
½ *teaspoon black pepper*

Shake well together and use as directed above.

BISTECCA MESSINESE
(Steak Messina Style)

Any 1 inch thick, boned steak (about 2 pounds)
1 *large thinly sliced onion*
1 *diced green pepper*
1 *cup chopped mushrooms*
1 *cup chopped celery*
1 *large diced carrot*
2 *diced potatoes*
2 *eight ounce cans tomato sauce or 1½ cups basic tomato sauce*

Dredge steak in flour and garlic powder, brown on both sides in small amount of olive oil. Then place in a baking pan. Add the remainder of the ingredients to the steak and bake at 325° for 2 hours.

STEAK PIZZAIOLA

> 1 recipe Pizzaiola sauce (p. 9)
> 3 thin steaks
> Salt and black pepper to taste
> Olive oil

Prepare the sauce. Season the steaks with salt and pepper and fry in a little olive oil until browned on each side and half cooked. Spread the sauce thickly over each steak, cover the pan and cook over low heat for 10 minutes.

Once you've tried this it will be hard to be satisfied with steak made in any other way.

BRACCIOLE means arms, and these tasty filled-rolled meat dishes do remind one of pudgy arms. They can be served just as they are, or along with the recipe for Mamma Bear's basic tomato sauce (p. 9), to dress up the plate of "gravy" meats that are served with macaroni or spaghetti. This can turn a poor man's dish into a King's delight. When these are served as the meat accompaniment to a great dish of macaroni, they are taken out of the sauce, sliced into ¼ inch pieces and arranged on a serving platter. This may be eaten along with the macaroni or spaghetti, or served as a separate meat course accompanied by vegetables and/or a crispy green salad.

BRACCIOLE DI MANZO
(Rolled Flank Steak)

> Flank steak
> Italian breadcrumbs
> Chopped Italian salami or pepperoni slices
> Hard-boiled egg, sliced

When you go to buy this cut at the supermarket, it may be designated as flank steak, steak for rolling, or Bracciola.

According to the size of cut you get and how large a Bracciola you want, the cooking time and method will differ. For a large Bracciola it will be best to bake them until brown in a 375° oven. For small ones, it is best to brown them in a skillet in ¼ cup of olive oil.

Roll out the beef and cover it with a generous coating of Italian breadcrumbs, chopped Italian salami or pepperoni slices and slices of hardboiled egg. Roll up carefully at a diagonal and fasten closed with strong toothpicks, cooking skewers, or cooking thread. Then brown in skillet if small or brown in oven if large.

Veal cutlets or chicken cutlets may also be used to make Bracciola. You prepare and cook them the same way as for beef Bracciola.

Early every Sunday morning Mamma rises to make the morning coffee and begin her tomato sauce. The usual addition to her sauce are her incomparable meatballs. For a long time every Sunday morning while she was in church, some of the meatballs would disappear from the pot. This was the mystery of the "Meatball Snatcher." One Sunday morning she decided to make the beds upstairs first and go to a later Mass. She heard someone come into the kitchen through the back door and a moment later heard the lid being removed from the pot of sauce. She knew it was the mysterious "Meatball Snatcher." She quietly came down the stairs and approached the kitchen. What she saw was my oldest brother Leo standing near the pot, lid in one hand and a speared meatball in the other, sinking his teeth into the juicy morsel while his grandson Eugene (seven years old) was sitting at the table and whispering to his grandfather: "Popi, can I have one?" Finally the mystery was solved. They all broke into laughter when Eugene displayed wisdom beyond his seven years as he declared: "Grandma, you make the best meatballs in the world! Can you give my mommy the recipe?"

When you begin to make these meatballs in your own home, don't be surprised if a mysterious "Meatball Snatcher" shows up in your kitchen.

POLPETTI DI MAMMATE
(Mamma's Meatballs)

> 2 *pounds ground chuck*
> 1¼ *cups breadcrumbs (Italian, as prepared on p. 35)*
> ½ *cup chopped parsley*
> 3 *cloves finely minced garlic or 1 teaspoon garlic powder*
> 2 *eggs*
> ¼ *cup water*
> 1 *cup grated Parmesan cheese*

Mix all ingredients together in bowl (with your hands of course. If you're squeamish, use a potato masher) and form into 1 inch balls. Fry until golden brown in olive oil. Eat as they are, or add them to Mamma Bear's tomato sauce and serve with spaghetti or macaroni.

Among the lists of charismatic gifts and ministries that St. Paul includes in his letters to the Corinthians, there is one that is conspicuous by its absence. I have no doubt that if Paul had been a guest in my mother's kitchen, he would have added to that list of charisms (free gifts God gives to the followers of His Son through the power of the Holy Spirit to enable them to minister to one another), the charismatic gift of good cooking. St. Paul would have learned from my mother, as I have, that what transforms these simple ingredients skillfully blended into joyous masterpieces, is that they are prepared and served with a generous amount of warm Christian love. A simple cup of water given to another for the love of Jesus becomes the most magnificent wine.

I believe that the next recipe is the most "charismatic" of all because of the time and love necessary to prepare it.

VEAL ALLA CALABRESE

> 2 *pounds veal cutlets*
> ½ *cup flour*
> ½ *teaspoon salt*
> ½ *teaspoon pepper*
> ¼ *cup olive oil*
> ½ *pound small fresh mushrooms*
> ½ *cup water*
> 2 *tablespoons white distilled vinegar*

Wash the cutlets under cold water and pat dry with a paper towel. Cut the meat into 2 inch strips and pound with a kitchen mallet. (This pounding tenderizes the veal.) Next dredge the veal strips in ½ cup flour seasoned with ½ teaspoon each of salt and pepper. Brown the strips quickly in ¼ cup olive oil. Remove the meat and set it aside. Sauté in the same oil ½ pound small fresh mushrooms that have been previously boiled for 5 minutes in salted water and drained. (2 large cans of small whole mushrooms may be used instead.)

Return the veal to the skillet and add ½ cup of water and 1 teaspoon of salt. Let simmer for ½ hour over low heat. Then add 2 tablespoons white distilled vinegar and simmer for another 10 minutes.

Serve over cooked rice.

Once you taste this dish, the only thing that will prevent you from having it three times a week is the outrageous price of veal.

Another delectable recipe for veal is this classic:

VEAL PARMIGIANA

Make veal cutlets according to recipe #1 under Italian breadcrumbs on page 36. In an oven dish or pan arrange cooked cutlets on a layer of basic tomato sauce (p. 9). Place slices of mozzarella (pizza cheese) on top of cutlets and cover with sauce. Cook in 350° oven for 10 minutes. Serve hot.

SALTIMBOCCA
(Veal—Roman Style)

> 2 pounds Italian style veal cutlets
> ½ pound prosciutto (imported Italian ham) or domestic boiled ham
> 1 pound mozzarella cheese (sliced domestic provolone can be used with equal success)
> ¼ cup olive oil
> 1 tablespoon butter
> 1 small thinly sliced onion
> Salt and pepper to taste
> ½ cup dry white wine

In frying pan, melt butter and add olive oil. Quickly brown the veal cutlets and remove. Add onion, salt and pepper to same pan and sauté until turning brown. (Be careful not to burn.) Then add wine and bring to a boil. Lower heat and stir, and simmer for 5 minutes.

In large oven pan, which has been lightly greased with butter, place the lightly browned veal cutlets, making sure each cutlet touches the bottom of the pan. Place a slice of ham on each cutlet, topped with a thin slice of cheese. Pour wine sauce over the contents of the pan, and place in 350° oven for

15 minutes or until cheese is melted and begins to brown slightly. Serve with boiled white rice for a Roman feast. This should serve 4 to 5 adults adequately.

There is a story about a typical American (Anglo-Saxon) who became interested in Italian food because her next-door neighbor was a generous Italian-American who always sent samples of her cooking over. One day, the Italian lady sent something over that the American family raved about. The American lady telephoned to find out what it was and to ask for the recipe. Her Italian neighbor said it was tripe and the only place it could be purchased was from a little butcher shop in the Italian section of town. If the American lady would go down there and buy a pound of it, her Italian neighbor would be happy to show her how to cook it. The poor American lady had no idea what tripe was, so she dutifully ventured down to the Italian butcher shop. What she saw nearly made her run out screaming. There in front of her on gleaming steel hooks she saw goats heads, eyes fixed in a stare, rabbits turned out of their skins, and baby calves skinned and gutted. She nervously waited her turn and asked almost in a whisper; "Do you have any tripe?"

"Sure" the butcher answered as he opened the showcase and pulled out a tray of white honey-combed substance with his blood-stained hands. "How much do you want?"

"One pound," she answered. "But first can you tell me what it is?"

The butcher looked at her for a moment. Then noticing her pale freckled complexion and light hair, he answered: "Lady, it's cow stomach!"

She couldn't speak for a moment, then finding her voice said: "Never mind, just give me a pound of ground meat." She took her package and left in a hurry.

She arrived home to her waiting family and said simply: "They didn't have any tripe."

This story merely points out that the Italians, like most other Europeans, eat with gusto foods that others would run away from. My advice is if you don't know what it is, ask, and if you don't think you'll like it, don't eat it. With that warning out of the way, let's make TRIPPA ALLA CALABRESE.

TRIPPA ALLA CALABRESE

> 1 *pound tripe*
> 1 *teaspoon black pepper or crushed red pepper*
> 1 *bay leaf*
> ½ *teaspoon oregano*
> 1 *large onion, thinly sliced*
> 4 *peeled potatoes, diced*
> 1 *cup water*
> 1 *eight ounce can tomato sauce*
> 1 *cup basic tomato sauce*
> ¼ *cup olive oil*

Cut the tripe into ¼ inch strips (scissors work well here). Wash well in salted water and rinse in clear water. Then put in pot and barely cover with water to which 1 tablespoon salt has been added. Add the pepper, bay leaf and oregano. Bring to a boil, then lower heat to simmer for ½ hour. Then add the onion and potatoes and cook until water evaporates. Then add the tomato sauce and olive oil, bring to a boil then lower heat and simmer for ½ hour.

BEEF STEW ITALIANA

> 2 *pounds stew beef, cubed*
> 4 *peeled and quartered potatoes*
> ½ *cup olive oil*
> 2 *thinly sliced onions*
> 2 *small cans tomato sauce or 2 cups basic tomato sauce*
> *Salt and pepper to taste*

Brown meat in ½ cup olive oil in large heavy saucepan. Remove meat and brown potatoes in same saucepan. Remove potatoes. Brown 2 thinly sliced onions in same saucepan. Then replace all ingredients along with two small cans tomato sauce or two cups basic tomato sauce. Salt and pepper to taste. Simmer over low heat for 2 hours adding water as needed.

It was a long-standing tradition in Italy for every little town to have an annual celebration or festa in honor of its patron saint. These feste were characterized by outdoor processions in which the statue or image of the patron saint was carried through the streets and into the village church in which a religious ceremony was held. The origins of these traditions go back to religion of pagan Italy, and the ceremonies which the people used to honor the gods and goddesses. When Christianity came to Italy, holy men and women, the saints, were honored because they had lived in heroic sanctity. The saint was venerated not because he or she was a little god, but because during his or her life, he or she demonstrated great virtues in practicing the Christian life. When they lived they were sought after by the common people because they consistently displayed charismatic gifts, such as healing or miracles. Even today, there are men and women whose ministries the Lord honors in remarkable ways, such as Kathryn Kuhlman and Father MacNutt, and who point out that it is not they who heal but the Lord. The ordinary Christian understands that all good comes from the Lord, yet when he comes upon a sanctified individual he regards them as special intercessors and honors them. Perhaps in the Roman Catholic world, enthusiasm carried veneration of these saints of God to almost the point of idolatry. The saints themselves expressed justified horror at the thought and were always careful to give all the glory to Jesus and to strenuously teach that the sanctified life was not their special privilege but available to all Christians who would give their lives completely to Jesus. They would say "Don't honor me, for I am just like you, but learn from me to follow Jesus."

When the Italians immigrated to this country and gathered in "Little Italies," they brought with them their long tradition of the festa. One of the traditional foods served at these celebrations of the saints' lives was the almost maddening sausage sandwich, maddening because it was so delicious. Here then is the recipe for:

SALCICCI DI FESTA
(Festive Sausage Sandwiches)

> 1 *pound sweet or hot Italian sausage cut into three inch lengths*
> 4 *green peppers, washed, and cut into ¼ inch strips*
> 3 *medium potatoes, peeled and quartered*
> 2 *medium onions, sliced thick*
> ¼ *cup olive oil*
> 1 *teaspoon salt*

Brown the sausage in a heavy skillet, then remove. Add olive oil, peppers, potatoes, onions and salt. Cook over low heat until all vegetables are tender. Place sausage in crisp Italian rolls and cover with pepper mixture. Bite in and enjoy *una buona festa* (a good feast).

CHICKEN ALLA WAX PAPER

This recipe is another Mamma Orsini original. It was invented in the days before aluminum foil, but amazingly the wax on the paper does not melt. When you serve it, you will be tempted to lick the paper; go ahead and lick to your heart's content, there's nothing wrong in really enjoying this delicious dish. If you were to patent it, you'd probably put the quick chicken people out of business.

2 fryers cup into pieces
1 recipe Italian breadcrumbs (p. 35)

Wash the chicken pieces and pat dry with a paper towel. Coat well with breadcrumbs. Place each piece of chicken on a sheet of wax paper large enough to wrap securely. Sprinkle with olive oil and wrap tightly. Place wrapped pieces in single layer, fold down, in large shallow oven pan. Bake in 375° oven for approximately 1 hour. Serve immediately.

This is another interesting way to serve budget chicken:

POLLO AL LIMONE
(Chicken with Lemon)

1 large cut up chicken
¼ cup olive oil
3 lemons, squeezed for all their juice
1 teaspoon salt
½ teaspoon black pepper

Wash chicken pieces thoroughly in clear cold water. Allow to dry. Place in oven pan. Mix together all the ingredients in a cup and pour over the chicken. Save some for basting.

If you add peeled and quartered potatoes to the pan, prepare a good salad, and you'll have a pleasant easy dinner.

Bake chicken in 375° oven for 45 minutes, basting with remaining lemon mixture. Serve hot.

Another chicken standby in Italian-American kitchens is:

CHICKEN ALLA CACCIATORE
(Hunter's Style)

> 3 *pound roasting chicken*
> 3 *tablespoons olive oil*
> 1 *medium onion, finely chopped*
> 1 *clove garlic, crushed*
> ⅝ *cup dry white wine*
> 12 *ounces ripe tomatoes, skinned and diced or 1 fourteen ounce can*
>   *peeled tomatoes, crushed*
> 1 *teaspoon tomato paste*
> ¼ *ounce teaspoon oregano*
> 4 *ounce button mushrooms, sliced*
> *Salt, pepper and sugar to taste*

Divide the chicken into 8 pieces. Heat the oil in a shallow sauce pan and fry the chicken over low heat for about 12 minutes or until golden on all sides. After 5 minutes add onion and garlic and fry with the chicken. Add wine and allow to bubble briskly until reduced by half then stir in the tomatoes, tomato paste and oregano. Cover the pan and simmer gently for 20 minutes. Add the mushrooms and seasoning to taste. Continue cooking gently, without the lid, for another 10 minutes or until mushrooms are cooked and tomatoes reduced to a sauce consistency. Serve hot with good Italian bread.

POLLO IMBRIACATO
(Chicken with Wine Sauce)

4 *large chicken breasts with bone*
4 *cloves of garlic, peeled and coarsely minced*
1 *cup water*
2 *cups wine (dry red)*
¼ *cup olive oil*
¼ *cup chopped parsley*
2 *large potatoes, peeled and quartered*
1 *tablespoon salt*
1 *teaspoon black pepper*

In large saucepan, brown chicken well in olive oil, then remove. Next brown potatoes, adding more oil if necessary, then remove. Lightly sauté garlic in same pot, add salt, pepper and parsley. Then add cooked chicken and potatoes. Simmer together for 5 minutes, add water and wine, bring to boil over medium heat, then simmer over low heat for 1 hour. Serve with crusty Italian bread (to sop up the delicious gravy) and a crisp green salad. This should serve four adults with hearty appetites.

Chapter 11
Fruits of the Sea

Not too long ago in the Roman Catholic world every Friday was fish-day. Meat was not eaten on Fridays as a sacrificial reminder to Catholic Christians that on Good Friday our Lord Jesus Christ made the supreme sacrifice of His life to save us all from our sins. There were other special days selected during the year, especially Christmas Eve, that were so honored. The tradition of the Christmas Eve abstinence from meat gave birth to the practice in Italian families of coming together to feast on fish.

I have selected a few fish recipes that are favorites in

Italian-American homes and are likely to become your favorites too.

PESCE STOCCO O BACCALA

2 pounds dried cod
2 medium onions, minced coarsely
2 large potatoes, peeled and quartered
2 fresh ripe tomatoes, washed and quartered
½ teaspoon salt
½ teaspoon crushed red pepper
¼ cup olive oil
Water

Soak the dried cod for 24 hours, changing the water about 6 times. Remove skin from the softened cod and separate the cod flesh from any bone with sharp knife. Cut the cod into large bite-size pieces. Place in collander to drain.

In heavy saucepan, sauté the onion in olive oil over low heat until soft. Slowly brown the potatoes in same pan. Remove. Add the fish, and sauté over medium heat for 10 minutes. Add salt, red pepper, tomatoes, and cooked potatoes. Stir gently. Add just enough cold water to cover contents of pan. Bring to a slow boil, then lower heat and allow to simmer for ½ hour. Serve in deep bowls with good Italian bread to soak up the gravy.

When I was a little kid during the immediate post-depression, my family lived in a modest rented second story. My mother frequently cooked the above dish on Fridays and because of its first stage of preparation, I could always tell when it was Thursday. Our bathroom was located at the head of the stairs leading to our front door and on Thursdays, there would always be a large dried cod fish floating in the bathtub.

The bathtub, fortunately for us kids who hated baths, was the only vessel large enough to contain the dried cod. One day, a little friend of mine who had never been inside my house, came to call me out to play. He saw two doors after he had climbed the stairs, one directly in front of him (the bathroom) and the other to his right (our front door). I was in the bathroom at the time having just washed my face and hands, and I heard a loud knock at the door. I opened the door and saw the shocked look of my little pal when he looked past me and saw the bathroom. Before I could hurry him into the other door, his swift eyes caught sight of that huge fish floating in the bathtub. His innocently sincere comment was "WOW! That's terrific! I bet you're the only kid on the block who can go fishing in his bathtub." Whenever I hear about Pesce Stocco o Baccala, I think about how neat it would be for a kid to go fishing in his bathtub.

SHRIMP SCAMPI

> 1 *pound raw fresh or frozen shrimp, shelled and cleaned*
> 6 *large garlic cloves, diced*
> ¼ *cup chopped parsley*
> 1 *teaspoon salt*
> ½ *teaspoon pepper*
> ¼ *cup olive oil*

Heat olive oil in large fry pan or saucepan. Sauté diced garlic until just turning brown. Add shrimp, salt and pepper. Mix and sauté over medium heat for 5 minutes. Add parsley and simmer covered for 15 minutes. Serve hot with slices of Italian bread to sop up the delicious soupy gravy.

PESCE ALLA PIZZAIOLA
(Fish with Tomato Sauce)

> 4 *portions any white fish, skinned and boned (frozen or fresh)*
> 1 *bay leaf*
> ½ *cup chopped parsley*
> ½ *teaspoon thyme*
> 5 *tablespoons olive oil*
> 1 *cup seasoned flour (mix 1 teaspoon salt, ½ teaspoon pepper and*
> ½ *teaspoon garlic powder into flour)*
> 2 *finely minced cloves of garlic*
> 1 *pound ripe tomatoes, peeled and chopped or 1 fourteen ounce can*
> *peeled tomatoes*
> *Salt, pepper and sugar to season*

Lay the fish with the bay leaf, parsley and thyme in a dish and pour the olive oil over it. Leave for 2 hours, turning the fish once. Drain and dry the fish, then coat with the seasoned flour. Strain the marinade into a fry pan and, when hot, fry the fish until golden on both sides and cooked, about 8–12 minutes depending on thickness. Drain the fish, arrange on a serving dish and keep hot. Add the garlic to the oil remaining in the pan and when the garlic is golden add the tomatoes and cook over high heat until the liquid is evaporated and tomatoes reduced to a thick pulpy sauce. Add salt, pepper and dash of sugar. Mix well and pour over fish. Serve immediately.

FRIED SHRIMP ITALIANO

> 1 *pound raw, shelled and de-veined shrimp*
> 1 *recipe frying batter (p. 5)*
> *Oil for frying*

Dip shrimp into batter and lower into hot oil. Fry from 4–8 minutes depending on size, until golden and crisp. Drain on absorbent paper and serve immediately.

BAKED FISH SICILIANO

> 3 *portions white fish, skinned and boned (halibut, tuna, cod, etc.)*
> 2 *tablespoons olive oil*
> 1 *medium onion, chopped*
> 1 *eight ounce can peeled tomatoes*
> 2 *cloves garlic, whole*
> 1 *teaspoon salt*
> ½ *teaspoon pepper*
> 8 *pitted green olives, chopped*
> 1 *tablespoon capers, drained*
> 1 *tablespoon chopped parsley*
> 1 *small stalk celery, very finely chopped*

Arrange the fish in single layer in an oiled shallow oven casserole. Heat the olive oil in a fry pan and sauté the onion gently until soft and golden. Add the canned tomatoes and their juice, the garlic, salt and pepper. Cook briskly stirring frequently for 5 minutes.

Stir in the olives, capers, parsley and celery and spoon sauce evenly over the fish. Cover and bake in 375° oven for 25 minutes. Serve hot.

MERLUZZO IN BRODETTO
(Whiting in Thin Sauce)

> 2 *pounds whiting cleaned and boned*
> 2 *cloves garlic, peeled and whole*
> ¼ *cup olive oil*
> ¼ *cup chopped parsley*
> 1 *teaspoon salt*
> ½ *teaspoon black pepper*
> 1 *cup of water*

In large saucepan, sauté garlic until golden over low heat. Add parsley, salt, pepper, and water and bring to a boil. Add the fish and simmer for 10 minutes. Serve in deep dishes accompanied with breadsticks of day-old Italian bread.

This dish is so digestible that old-timers from Italy say that it's great for sick people as well as those in the bloom of health. I have no doubt that once you try it, it will appear regularly on your family menu.

ZUPPA DI PESCE
(Fish Stew)

> *5 tablespoons olive oil*
> *1 onion, thinly sliced*
> *1 stalk celery, thinly sliced*
> *2 cloves garlic, crushed*
> *1 tablespoon chopped parsley*
> *1 eight ounce can peeled tomatoes, chopped*
> *⅓ cup white wine*
> *1¼ cups water*
> *1 teaspoon salt*
> *½ teaspoon pepper*
> *1 small mackerel, gutted and trimmed*
> *8 ounce piece halibut*
> *2 fillets lemon sole*
> *6 ounces small frozen shrimp, thawed*
> *Handful each mussels and clams, cleaned and in shells (optional)*

Heat the oil in large saucepan over low heat and fry the onion, garlic and celery until soft and golden. Add parsley, tomatoes, wine, water, salt and pepper. Simmer for 15 minutes. Meanwhile skin the fish, cut mackerel into thick slices, halibut into bite-size chunks, and sole into strips 1 inch wide. Add all to the broth, with a little more water if necessary and simmer gently for 10 minutes. Add shrimp (and shell fish if desired) and cook for another 5 minutes. Pour fish stew over grilled thick slices of Italian bread in large bowls. Should serve about four.

Chapter 12

Golden Eggs without the Goose

Most of these recipes were tested and enjoyed in the warm Christian atmosphere of Mr. and Mrs. Dan Hughes' kitchen. That's right, Hughes! Not *all* my friends are Italian. In fact, Dan and Ann Hughes, their daughter Patti and son Danny, are my official Pine Hill family. They were designated so by the *BOSS*, Mamma Orsini, after she met them. Danny is my disciple and traveling companion. My Italian nationality doesn't have *too* much influence on him, its only *coincidence* that when not in school (where he's studying Italian), he works part time at the *Naples Pizzeria* in Deptford Township, New Jersey. Again its only *coincidence* that the Pizzeria is owned and operated by a former student of mine, Anthony Pullella.

When I was putting this book together, Dan, Sr. suggested I include what was referred to in his boyhood days in Philadelphia as the "Depression Sandwich." It was referred to in this manner because it didn't cost much to make, was delicious, and kept body and soul together. So here it is, the "Depression Sandwich" or

PEPPERS AND EGGS

4 *large green peppers, washed and cut into* ¼ *inch strips*
1 *medium onion, sliced thin*
6 *eggs*
½ *cup Parmesan cheese*
1 *teaspoon salt*
½ *teaspoon black pepper*

Sauté peppers and onion in skillet until soft. Beat eggs, cheese, salt and pepper together and pour over pepper mixture. Cook until eggs are set but not too firm. Spoon into split hard crusted Italian rolls and watch as "depression" disappears.

FRITTATA CALABRESE
(Potato Omelet)

> 4 large diced potatoes
> 2 minced garlic cloves
> ½ cup chopped parsley
> 1 tablespoon salt
> 1 teaspoon pepper
> ½ cup olive oil
> 6 slightly beaten eggs
> ¾ cup grated Parmesan cheese

Brown potatoes and garlic in large skillet over medium heat. Lightly beat eggs with remaining ingredients and pour over browned potatoes. Reduce heat and cook until eggs are set around edges of skillet. Place under broiler until eggs are set on top and very lightly browned.

UOVA ROSATI
(Red Eggs)

> 6 eggs
> 4 medium ripe tomatoes
> 4 whole cloves of garlic
> ¼ cup olive oil
> 1 teaspoon salt
> ½ teaspoon crushed red pepper
> ½ cup grated Parmesan cheese

Sauté garlic, salt and red pepper in skillet until garlic begins to brown. Add tomatoes and crush with fork, mix well and simmer over low heat for ½ hour.

Beat eggs well with Parmesan cheese and pour into tomatoes, stirring mixture until eggs are cooked. Spoon onto plates, serve with crispy Italian bread and enjoy.

ASPARAGUS FRITTATA

> ¼ cup olive oil
> 1 finely chopped onion
> 1 finely chopped clove garlic
> 1 pound cooked asparagus spears
> 1 tablespoon lemon juice
> 6 slightly beaten eggs
> ¾ cup grated Parmesan cheese
> Salt and pepper to taste

In a large skillet sauté onion and garlic in oil, add asparagus. Spears should be arranged like spokes of a wheel. Sprinkle asparagus with lemon juice. Combine eggs and cheese, pour over asparagus; cook over low heat until eggs are set around edge of skillet. Place under broiler until eggs are set on top and slightly brown.

ASPARAGUS PIEMONTESE

> 1 pound cooked asparagus spears
> ¼ cup olive oil
> ½ cup grated provolone cheese
> 4 fried eggs
> 4 slices Italian toasted bread
> ½ cup grated Parmesan cheese
> ¼ cup chopped parsley
> Salt and pepper to taste

In a fry pan heat asparagus over medium heat in oil. Add provolone cheese, reduce heat, cover until cheese melts. Arrange toast on plates, cover with asparagus and place a fried egg on top. Sprinkle eggs with grated Parmesan and chopped parsley.

FRITTATA DI CIPOLLE
(Onion Omelet)

> 3 *large onions, sliced*
> 4 *tablespoons olive oil*
> 8 *eggs*
> *Salt and pepper to taste*
> ¼ *cup grated Parmesan cheese*
> ¼ *cup white vinegar*

Parboil the sliced onions in boiling salted water for a few minutes. Drain well and then sauté in large fry pan with butter. Beat the eggs in a bowl, adding salt, pepper, and grated cheese, pour them over the onions which have been well spread out over the bottom of the pan. When the eggs have become firm turn the omelet out onto a hot plate and sprinkle with vinegar. This should serve six very well.

Chapter 13

Nuns Don't Just Pray

As a child my first impression of Catholic nuns was that of severe-faced women dressed in long terrifying black dresses. They represented the dark and ominous side of Christianity and were to be treated with the greatest long-distance respect. They were to be revered because they were special supra-normal women who talked to God and taught children to fear Him. Much to my delight, I later discovered that they are normal ordinary women who have given their lives in service to God's people out of love for Jesus Christ. Nuns or sisters are wonderful women and so very very human, and I have been fortunate through the years to have many as my friends and associates in the Lord's vineyard.

The parish where I presently have residence is blessed

enough to have seven nuns to staff its parochial school. As resident in the parish rectory it falls to me to walk over to the convent chapel every weekday morning for 6:30 A.M. Mass. To fulfill this duty I have to rise every morning at 5:50 A.M. to shower, shave and wake up before I get there. Some mornings, especially after a long night of correcting papers and preparing for my own classes, only my body gets over to the convent. But when I realize that the Sisters have been in their chapel since 5:30 A.M. praying (probably for me), I try my best not to fall asleep while I'm reading to them from the Scriptures.

I forgot to mention that every sister except one is a native born Italian and they belong to the group of sisters called the Sisters of Our Lady of Mercy. Of course, the priests are invited often (not often enough to suit me!) to the convent to join the sisters for wonderful Italian dinners and warm Christian fellowship. They are delightful, witty, and wise good Christian women supremely dedicated to their task.

This next group of recipes was generously given to me by Mother Grazia, their immediate superior, at my insistence. I am going to give them as they were given to me, in Italian, but don't worry, I'll translate them for you. I wouldn't want you to miss out on these mouth-watering recipes.

RISOTTO IN BIANCO

Mettete in un tegame del burro con cipolla che farete rosolare. Quando questa é ben rosolata aggiungetevi il riso, che farete rosolare per circa un minuto e poi ci aggiungete un mezzo bicchiere di vino bianco. Quando questo è evaporato aggiungete del brodo di carne che avete preparato in precedenza, e fate cuocere per circa venti minuti senza toccarlo. (il brodo deve essere tre volte la quantitá del riso. es. 3 tazze di brodo e una di riso)

RISOTTO IN BIANCO
(Rice in White)

  1 *onion, thinly sliced*
  ½ *stick butter*
  1 *cup uncooked rice*
  ½ *cup white wine*
  3 *cups beef stock*

Sauté the onion in a saucepan into which ½ stick of butter has been melted. When the onion is beginning to brown, add 1 cup of uncooked rice, sauté for one minute, then add ½ cup of white wine. When the wine has evaporated, add 3 cups of beef stock. (You can make the beef stock yourself, or used canned clear beef stock.) Let this cook over low heat for 20 minutes. Serve hot.

POMODORI AL FORNO

Si tagliano i pomodori a fette piuttosto grosse e si dispongono in una teglia. Si metta sopra pane grattugiato, aglio, sale, prezzemolo e olio piuttosto abbondante e si fanno cuocere per circa un quarto d' ora. Si servono freddi e caldi. (I pomodori devono essere piuttosto acerbi).

ROASTED TOMATOES

Cut not so ripe tomatoes into thick slices. Place them in a shallow oven pan. Generously sprinkle with Italian bread-crumbs (p. 35) and olive oil. Let them cook in 350° oven for 15 minutes. Serve hot or cold.

FUNGHI RIPIENI

Togliere ai funghi il gambo e parte dell'interno. Spellarli e tritarli con la mezzaluna. Preparare un battuto con prezzemolo, poco aglio e metterlo in un tegame con olio e un fiocco di burro. Appenna il prezzemolo comincia a soffriggere mettete i gambi tritati. Fate insaporire per qualche minuto e poi aggiungete sale, pepe e altre spezie e un po di pane grattugiato e mescolate fino a che tutto sia ben amalgamato. Togliete dal fuoco il tegame e quando il contenuto e quasi freddo, aggiungete un po di formaggio grattugiato e unuova. Disponete una teglia con burro e mettete i cappelli dei funghi riempiti con il preparato, e coperti con una fettinz di mozzarella, o un fiocchetto di burro. Mettere a forno moderato per circa 25 minuti.

STUFFED MUSHROOMS

Large mushrooms
¼ cup of parsley
1 clove of garlic
Salt and pepper to taste
¼ cup breadcrumbs
⅛ cup grated Parmesan cheese
1 egg
Mozzarella cheese

Wash the mushrooms, remove the stems and mince them. Chop the parsley and garlic together, and sauté both in a mixture of olive oil and a pat of butter. As soon as the parsley begins to fry, add the minced mushroom stems. Let this simmer for a minute and then add salt and pepper to taste along with ¼ cup breadcrumbs. Mix until you have a pasty consistency. Remove from heat. When cool, add ⅛ cup grated Parmesan cheese and one egg. Mix well. Fill the mushroom caps with the mixture. Grease a shallow oven pan with butter and place the filled mushroom caps in it. Cover each stuffed cap with a small slice of mozzarella cheese or dot of butter. Bake in 300° oven for 25 minutes.

CARCIOFI RIPIENI
(Stuffed Artichokes)

Artichokes
¼ *cup olive oil*
⅛ *cup butter*

Filling

¼ *cup parsley*
2 *cloves minced garlic*
½ *pound ground beef*
1 *tablespoon tomato sauce*
Salt and pepper to taste
1 *cup beef or chicken stock*

Sauté ¼ cup parsley and two cloves minced garlic in butter. Crumble in ½ pound ground beef, salt and pepper to taste, and one tablespoon of tomato sauce (p. 9). Simmer until well cooked.

Remove the outer leaves and the choke from the artichokes. Wash and drain them completely. Fill them, and place them in a large saucepan in which ¼ cup of olive oil and ⅛ cup of butter have been heated. Cook them over low heat. Add about a cup of good beef or chicken stock (enough to cover bottoms of artichokes 1 inch). Cover and simmer for about ½ hour or until leaves pull off easily.

BOCCONCINI SAPORITI

Prendere delle fettine di vitella, impanarle a farle friggere nel burro misto con olio. Prendete una pirofila e ungerla con burro. Tagliare la carne a dadini e disporla nella pirofila a strati. Su ogni pezzetto di carne posare un pezzetto di prosciutto crudo o cotto ed un pezzetto di mozzarella, qualche pezzettino di burro e farlo cuocere nel forno a fuoco moderato per circa dieci minuti.

TASTY MOUTHFULS

Thin veal cutlets
Italian or boiled ham
Mozzarella cheese
Egg
Italian breadcrumbs
Olive oil
Butter

Take thin veal cutlets and dip first in slightly beaten egg and then in Italian breadcrumbs (p. 35). Brown them in olive oil and butter. Grease a baking dish with butter. Cut the cooked veal into 2 inch strips and place in a baking dish. Place on each strip of veal a 2 inch strip of Italian ham (prosciutto) or boiled ham and a 2 inch strip of sliced mozzarella cheese. Dot with butter and make another layer the same way on top. Place in 350° oven 10 minutes. Serve hot.

Chapter 14

Salad Ain't Limp Lettuce

INSALATA
(Italian Salads)

Italians eat light salads at the *end* of the meal, rather than at the beginning. The philosophy is that the fresh greens should follow the main course as a natural aid to good digestion. Light salads are simple affairs, perhaps torn fresh-crisp romaine or iceberg lettuce, lightly tossed with a mixture of olive oil and red wine vinegar, salt and pepper to taste. A good light salad dressing would consist of the following:

> ¼ *cup olive oil*
> 3 *tablespoons red wine vinegar*
> ½ *teaspoon salt*
> *Dash of pepper (sprinkle of oregano, optional)*

Shake well together and toss lightly with lettuce, escarole, endive or dandelion torn into small pieces.

During the summer, a fresh salad ranging from the simple to the complex, served with thick crisp and crusty slices of Italian bread can make a whole delightful meal. We will start with the simple and go on down to the more complex with variations.

INSALATA DI POMIDORI
(Tomato Salad)

> *5 medium, fresh vine-ripened red tomatoes, washed and quartered*
> *1 large onion, thinly sliced*
> *Salt, pepper (black or red crushed), and oregano to taste*
> *¼ cup olive oil*

Toss lightly all ingredients together.

INSALATA DI PATATE
(Potato Salad)

> *6 large potatoes boiled in skin*
> *2 medium onions thinly sliced*
> *⅔ cup olive oil*
> *¼ cup red wine vinegar*
> *2 teaspoons salt*
> *1 teaspoon black or red crushed pepper*

Peel potatoes when cooled and cut into large bite size chunks. Toss together lightly with other ingredients.

INSALATA SUPREMA
(Salad Supreme)

Follow the recipe for potato salad above then add:
> *1 can drained chick peas*
> *1 can Italian tuna fish or regular tuna packed in oil*
> *½ cup pitted black olives, sliced*
> *½ cup pitted green olives, sliced*
> *½ cup shredded mild Italian cheese (provolone or Bel Paese)*

Toss together well. Served in large portions with good Italian bread this makes a tasty light meal. It may also be served in smaller portions on beds of crisp lettuce, escarole or endive to make an excellent antipasto (appetizer).

Chapter 15

Dessert Ain't Just Sugar

One of the more popular feast days among Italian-Americans is the feast of St. Joseph, the foster father of Jesus. What little one reads concerning Joseph in the New Testament does inspire admiration for his courage and faith. When he took Mary to be his wife, she was already with child by the power of the Holy Spirit. Now this was a man whose love for God overcame the natural suspicion of human nature. His faithfulness and stewardship were and are beautiful models for Christian Fathers, even celibate priests called "Father." This brings up an interesting question that has been asked of me by many sincere fundamentalistic interpreters of the Scriptures. I am often asked "why do you allow yourself to be called Father, when the Lord said 'Call no man father upon earth, for you have one father, your heavenly Father.'" I have been often tempted to answer, "I'd rather be called Father than Daddy-o!" But the real answer I believe is this. When the Lord spoke those words He wasn't speaking literally. What He meant, I believe, was that we should never forget our origin in the creative power of God the Father and to remember that our earthly fathers were not the origin of our life, but that God is the origin of life, regardless of the biological intermediary causes. Be that as it may, let's return to the feast of St. Joseph. The Italians have always had a great admiration for him and his feast day, March 19. They have traditionally prepared and eaten the following rich dessert to commemorate St. Joseph's own richness of faith.

ZEPPOLE DI SAN GIUSEPPE
(St. Joseph's Feast Day Dessert)

> ½ *cup butter*
> *Dash salt*
> 1 *cup water*
> 1 *cup pastry flour*
> 4 *eggs*
> 1 *tablespoon sugar*
> ½ *teaspoon grated orange peel*
> ½ *teaspoon grated lemon peel*

Combine butter, salt and water in saucepan and bring to boil. Add flour all at one time, mix well until dough leaves sides of pan. Remove from stove and cool a little. Add eggs one at a time and mix well after each. Add sugar and grated peels and mix thoroughly.

Drop by tablespoonfuls on greased baking sheet leaving a 3-inch space between them. Bake in hot oven (400°) 10 minutes. Reduce heat to 325° and bake 30 minutes (yield 16). Partially split puffs and fill with the following:

> *Filling:*

> 1 *pound ricotta (Italian cottage cheese)*
> 2 *tablespoons chocolate chips*
> 1 *tablespoon candied orange peel*
> 2 *tablespoons sugar*

Mix well and fill puffs.

The fondest memories of the first six years of my life are of Papa, my father. I can remember gathering with my brothers and sister on cold winter mornings before the coal stove in our kitchen. Mamma would be pouring hot sugared coffee into bowls half-filled with heated milk, and Papa would be opening a brown bag filled with Biscotti (delicious hard cookies) he had baked the night before. We would each be given a steaming bowl of coffee, and a handful of the cookies to be dunked whole or broken into the bowl, and take our places before the warmth of the stove. I would take the honored position due me because I was the youngest, right on Papa's lap. In gratitude to Almighty God we would eat our simple breakfast and prepare for the day.

Mamma always declared that Papa was the real cook of the family and that she learned all she knew from him. He was a good man and an exemplary Christian, so when he left us to go with the Lord and await the Resurrection, he left us not only his Biscotti, but the strength of his Christian faith as an example for our lives.

It is in honor of his memory I give this next recipe:

PAPA'S COOKIES

> 4 eggs
> 1 cup sugar
> ½ cup oil or margarine
> 3 caps of vanilla
> 4 tablespoons baking powder
> 5 cups flour

Cream eggs and sugar, add shortening and vanilla, then:

Sift together 4 tablespoons baking powder and 2 cups of flour, add to wet ingredients and mix. Then add another 2 cups of flour gradually. Pour out on floured surface and knead adding approximately 1 more cup of flour. Knead until dough doesn't stick to your hands. Take slice of dough and roll out. Cut into strips and roll with fingers into any desired shape. Place on greased cookie sheet and bake at 350–375° oven for 12 minutes or more till golden brown.

MOSTARDA
(Grape Pudding)

This is one of Mamma's special recipes. It is made in September when the backyard grapes are ripe.

> *Fresh Concord grapes*
> *2 cups sugar*
> *1 cup water*
> *Rind from one orange*
> *3 cups Farina*
> *1 cup chopped walnuts*
> *1 cup semi-sweet chocolate bits*

Stem and wash enough Concord grapes to almost fill a 3 quart saucepan. Cover and allow to come to a boil over low heat. Simmer 15 to 20 minutes. Put cooked grapes into strainer and catch juice in bowl. Then grind grapes through food mill into a bowl containing the juice. Set aside.

In another saucepan boil 2 cups of sugar in 1 cup of water. Remove from heat and add the orange rind.

To the cooled grape juice add 3 cups of Farina and stir to dissolve. Add this mixture to the saucepan containing sugar syrup. Bring to boil over low heat stirring constantly until thick. Remove from heat and stir in the chopped walnuts and chocolate bits.

Test for sweetness. If more sugar is needed, add it now. Pour into dessert dishes, allow to cool and serve.

PASTERA

The greatest event in the history of mankind is the Resurrection of Jesus Christ that is celebrated each year on Easter Sunday. The reason why the Passion, Death, and Resurrection of Jesus were the greatest events in man's history, is because through the Paschal mystery men were freed from the bonds of sin and death and were enabled to become once again the Sons of God and heirs of heaven.

The main ingredient of the following Easter pie is wheat. Jesus himself told us the parable about the grain of wheat which must die and be buried in order that it may burst into new life. The grain of wheat was the symbol of His own death and resurrection. Wheat again was chosen by Him to be the everlasting memorial in the form of unleavened bread in the greatest Sacrament of His love and sacrifice, the Lord's Supper or Holy Communion.

Our recipe for wheat pie then is a fitting symbol of all our Lord has done and continues to do for us, His children.

PASTERA
(Easter Grain Pie)

Pie Crust:

5½ cups flour
3 teaspoons baking powder
½ teaspoon salt
1 cup sugar
1 cup shortening
1 cup water
1 unbeaten egg

Mix dry ingredients together, add the rest and mix well. Turn out onto lightly floured surface and knead till smooth. Form into two balls, one large for lower crust, one to form strips to cover top of pie. Cover and set aside.

Filling:

3½ pounds ricotta pot cheese
1 pound wheat (available from Italian stores)
1½ cups sugar
6 unbeaten eggs
1 tablespoon cinnamon
1 tablespoon vanilla
½ teaspoon salt
½ cup chopped candied citrus

Mix cheese, wheat and sugar. Fold in eggs one at a time. Add rest of ingredients and mix well. Pre-heat oven to 350°.

Roll out large ball of dough to 14 inches in diameter and ⅛ inch thickness. Place in ungreased spring pan. (12 inch) and add filling.

Roll out second ball of dough and cut into 1 inch wide strips. Criss-cross top of pie with strips. Brush with melted butter. Bake 2½ hours till golden brown.

There is one acknowledged "expert" of the culinary arts in the Orsini family, and that is my brother Leo's wife, my sister-in-law, Inez. She is an excellent cook, a marvelous baker, and a great hostess at holiday dinner parties. Every holiday, the Orsini clan gathers around Inez's dessert table at the end of the evening to partake of the scrumptious delicacies only she can prepare. I persuaded her to share her dessert secrets with us so that your gatherings can be as sweet and delicious as ours. We begin with an Italian wine punch that goes well with sweets:

VINO DOLCE E SPUMANTE

1 bottle Asti Spumanti wine	(1 quart)	cold
1 bottle inexpensive rosé wine	(1 quart)	cold
1 bottle club soda	(1 quart)	cold
1 bottle ginger ale	(1 quart)	cold
1 package lemon ice	(1 quart)	frozen
1 package frozen strawberries		thawed

In a large punch bowl, pour all liquid ingredients over the lemon ice, and garnish with the thawed strawberries. Serve this beautiful punch with the following specialties:

CRISPELLE

2 cups all-purpose flour
3 eggs
¼ cup sugar

Place flour and sugar in a mixing bowl, mix thoroughly, then form a little well in its center. Add the eggs one at a time, mixing well (use the original mixer—your hands). Place the dough you have made on a floured surface and knead for 10 minutes. Cut the dough in half and knead each half for another 10 minutes. Allow the dough to rest for 10 minutes, and then roll one of the halves with a rolling pin on a floured surface until very thin. With a pastry cutter, cut into ¾ inch strips. Do the same thing with the second half of dough. Fry the strips in 2 inches of very hot oil until browned. Drain on brown paper and sprinkle with powdered sugar or, as an interesting alternative for the topping, you can boil 2 ounces of water, add 4 ounces of honey and bring to a boil. Once the mixture has cooled it can be spooned over the crispelle.

BISCOTTI A L'ANICE
(Anisette Biscuits)

3 cups all-purpose flour
3 teaspoons baking powder
1 cup sugar
½ teaspoon salt
½ cup shortening
3 eggs
2 ounces anisette

Cream shortening and add sugar; beat until creamy. Add eggs one at a time, beating well after each addition. Stir in sifted dry ingredients, and add the anisette. Mix well. Shape into 4 loaves. Place on lightly greased cookie sheet and bake for 35 minutes at 350 degrees. When baked, remove from oven and place immediately on a cutting board. Cut into ½ inch slices. Place slices, cut side up, on baking sheet and place in low heated oven to toast. Turn them to toast both sides. Remove, cool and serve.

BISCOTTI REGINA
(Italian Sesame Cookies)

4 cups flour
1 teaspoon baking powder
1 cup sugar
1 cup shortening
¼ cup orange juice
4 eggs
1½ teaspoons vanilla
Sesame seeds

Sift dry ingredients together, add shortening and mix very well. Add the juice, eggs, and vanilla, and mix together. Turn out on floured surface and form into a long loaf. Slice off 2 inch strips and roll each strip in a mixture of beaten egg and ¼ cup of milk. Roll the strips in sesame seeds and place on a lightly greased cookie sheet. Place the sheet into a 400° oven for 18 to 20 minutes. Remove, cool and serve.

To complete your holiday table, we have the two best saved for last:

CASSATA DI FESTA
(Holiday Delight)

> 6 *eggs*
> 1 *cup sugar*
> 1 *cup flour*

Crack eggs into bowl of electric mixer and beat at medium speed for 20 minutes, adding one teaspoon of sugar at a time until all is used, but in the first 10 minutes. Next add 1 tablespoon of flour at a time for the final 10 minutes. Pour the batter into two lightly greased 9 inch layer tins lined with wax paper. Bake 20 minutes at 350 degrees. Remove and cool.

> *Filling:*
>
> 1½ *pounds ricotta cheese*
> 1 *cup sugar*
> 1 *small jar candied fruits*
> 1 *small almond chocolate bar broken into bits*
> ¼ *cup water*

Beat cheese and sugar together and reserve 1 cup of mixture. Add the fruits and chocolate to the remainder. Mix well. Now split each baked cake into 2 layers. Place first layer on a serving dish and brush with crème de cocoa; spread ¼ of the filling over the layer and repeat the process with the remaining 3 layers. On top of the last layers, spread a thin icing made of ¼ cup of water and enough confectioner's sugar to proper consistency. Finally, cover the sides with the reserved cup of ricotta filling. Fit for a king!

PIGNOLATA
(Honey Drops)

> 2½ *pound box prepared biscuit flour (Bisquick)*
> ½ *cup sugar*
> 1 *cup milk*
> 2 *eggs*
> 1 *cup honey*

In a large mixing bowl, combine flour, sugar, milk and eggs. Mix well. The resulting dough will be of a thick consistency. Turn out onto a lightly floured surface and knead until dough can be rolled between the hands without falling apart. If dough is too loose, add a few drops of water to thicken its consistency. Take enough dough from the mass to fit into the palm of the hand. Roll into long cylinder about ½ inch thick, and cut off ½ inch bits from the rolled cylinder of dough. Treat all of the dough in the same way.

Melt 2 cups of shortening in a deep fryer and bring to high heat. Place a strainer that fits within the dimensions of the deep-fryer and drop a small handful of the dough bits at a time into the hot grease. Fry the bits until golden brown, remove with strainer and place in absorbent paper. Continue this frying process until all the dough bits are fried.

Arrange the fried bits in a mound on a serving dish and pour to cover with honey. Serve by placing a large spoonful on cake dishes. These are eaten with a teaspoon.

These are a Christmas season favorite around our house.

Chapter 16

Alla Casalinga

In the Italian tradition, families are noted for their conspicuous attitudes of loyalty and allegiance to their immediate members and the strong customs that govern family life. Even in the modern Italian-American family there exists a strict "order of the family" that is usually observed even by the third and fourth generations. This "order of the family" views the family unit as central to the life of each individual, and it is characterized by a complex structure of rules regarding the roles of each member of the family. Also involved in this conception of family life are the traditional concepts of family honor, pragmatic attitudes toward sex and religion, and a regard for food as the host of life.

Traditionally, the home is the site and the source of all that gives meaning to life. To an Italian a well-kept home is the symbol of a sound family. Furniture that lasts is symbolic of family stability and hence family strength. Perhaps most important of all, plentiful food, carefully prepared, is a sign of family well-being.

When I was a child food was symbolic in a real way of the love my family had for me. It was the product of the labor of my father and brothers, and it was prepared for us with care by my mother. It was, in a very emotional sense, a connection with my father and mother and symbolic of their outreach to me. In a very poignant way, meals were a communion of the family and food was sacred because it was a medium of that communion. I believe that this attitude towards food and meals is characteristically shared by most Italians and it is one of the reasons why they consider the practice of saying a short prayer before meals to be unnecessary. As one Italian woman said to me, "The food comes from God, it's already blessed, it keeps us together; why bless it again?"

True, these values had their origins in times that were far less rushed and hectic than ours. But they are values well worth retaining, since they represent a positive and stabilizing influence.

The recipes I have included here come from the tradition that I have described above, a tradition which can become a part of every Christian family.

Chapter 17

COMMON INGREDIENTS AND TERMS IN ITALIAN COOKING

Al Burro	Dressed with butter
Al Dente	Not over-cooked; firm-textured pasta
Al Forno	Cooked in the oven
Al'Aceto	In vinegar
Alla Casalinga	Home style
Alla Marinara	Seaman style
Arrosto	Roast meat
Asparagi	Asparagus
Baccalà	Dried salt cod
Basilico	Sweet basil
Bel Paese	Semi-soft mild cheese
Biscotto	Biscuit
Bistecca	Beefsteak
Bracciolo	Meat for rolling and stuffing
Brodo	Broth
Caffè Latte	Coffee with milk

Caffè Espresso	Black 'espresso' coffee
Cannelloni	Large round pasta often served stuffed
Capperi	Capers
Carciofi	Artichokes
Cassata	Rich cake
Cavolfiore	Cauliflower
Cavolo	Cabbage
Cipolla	Onion
Coppa	Cup
Costoletta	Cutlet
Crudo	Raw or uncooked
Ditali	Short tubular pasta
Ditallini	A small variety of the above
Dolce	General term for pudding
Fagiolini	Fresh or dried beans
Farina Bianca	White wheat flour
Fegato	Liver
Fettucine	Home-made narrow ribbon pasta
Filetto	Thin fillet of meat or fish
Finocchio	Fennel
Formaggio	Cheese
Frittata	Omelette
Frittelle	Pancakes. Also used for fritters.
Fritto Misto	Mixture of fried foods
Frutti Di Mare	Small shellfish
Funghi	Mushrooms
Gamberi	Shrimp
Gelato	Frozen—usually ice cream
Imbottiti	Stuffed

Involtini	Slice of meat stuffed and rolled
Insalata	Salad
Lasagne	Wide flat noodles
Latte	Milk
Lesso	Boiled
Limone	Lemon
Maccheroni	Generic term for all types of pasta
Maiale	Pork
Manzo	Beef
Melanzane	Egg plant
Minestra	Soup. Also generic term for pasta or rice course
Minestrone	Thick vegetable soup
Mozzarella	Soft white unsalted cheese
Olio	Oil
Oliva	Olive
Origano	Herb used for flavoring Oregano
Pane	Bread
Pane Abbrustolito	Toasted bread
Panna	Cream
Parmigiano	Hard cheese much used in Italian cookery. Parmesan.
Pasta	Dough. Generic name for all macaroni products
Pasta Asciutto	Pasta served with butter or a sauce
Pasta in Brodo	Pasta cooked in broth and served as soup
Pasticceria	General term for pastry
Pecorino	Strong sheep's milk cheese

Peperone	Sweet peppers
Peperoncini	Small hot peppers
Pesce	Fish
Pignoli	Pine nuts
Polenta	Corn meal
Pollo	Chicken
Polpette	Small meat balls
Polpettone	Large meat loaf
Pomodori	Tomatoes
Prezzemolo	Parsley
Prosciutto	Ham
Provolone	A hard yellow cheese
Ravioli	Stuffed squares of pasta
Ricotta	Soft curd cheese, 'pot cheese'
Rigatoni	Large grooved macaroni
Ripieno	Stuffed or stuffing
Riso	Rice
Risotto	Rice dish
Salsa	Sauce
Salsiccia	Generic term for sausage
Scalloppine	Thin small slices of veal
Scampi	Large shrimp
Sedano	Celery
Spaghetti	Thin varieties of pasta
Spinaci	Spinach
Spumante	Sparkling wine
Sugo	Sauce
Tagliatelle	Home-made ribbon pasta
Tonno	Tuna fish

Torrone	A type of nougat candy
Torta	Generic term for cake
Tortellini	A stuffed pasta
Trippa	Tripe
Uova	Eggs
Uva	Grapes
Verdure	Vegetables
Vermicelli	Very small spaghetti
Vino	Wine
Vitello	Veal
Vongole	Clams
Zita	Tubular shape pasta
Zucchini	Squash
Zuppa	Soup

Some Pasta Terms

Pasta in brodo	Pasta served in broth
Pasta secca	Eggless pasta
Pasta all'uova	Egg pasta
Pasta fatta in casa	Home-made pasta
Pasta verde	Green (spinach) pasta
Pastini	Small soup shapes
Maccheroni	Generic term for pasta

GENERAL INFORMATION

When cooking pasta choose a large pan.

Allow plenty of water, about 4 pints for 12 ounces pasta.

Add 1 level teaspoon salt per pint water. Wait for a full rolling boil before putting pasta in water.

Add pasta gradually, stirring a few times. If using long spaghetti or macaroni, coil it around inside the pan as it softens.

Keep the water boiling and cook without a lid.

Do not overcook. Pasta should be tender but firm to the teeth (al dente).

Cooking times vary according to type and size of pasta. Note label recommendations and use the "bite" test.

When cooked to your liking immediately remove from heat, adding a cup of cold water to stop further cooking.

Drain thoroughly in a colander.

Turn into a heated dish and toss with a little butter or olive oil.

Serve with previously prepared sauce.

QUANTITIES

For main dishes allow about 3 ounces pasta per person. For soups 4 ounces pasta to 1½–2 pints soup. On average expect pasta to double its volume when cooked.

Index